Child-Adolescent Behaviour

This book briefly outlines psychological perspectives of the values, attitudes and behaviour of parents in influencing a child's personality. The volume discusses important factors and family surroundings that influence a growing child's development and various techniques that parents and teachers may use to inculcate children's growth and well-being. Various discipline techniques that parents can use with the child and ways in which they can enhance their child's creativity and achievement levels are explained. It also discusses the causes, signs and types of learning disabilities, such as dyslexia, dysgraphia, dyscalculia and developmental coordination disorder (dyspraxia), and behaviour disorders like anxiety disorders, conduct disorders, oppositional defiant disorder, attention-deficit hyperactivity disorder (ADHD), aggressive behaviour in children and the speech disorder stuttering. The volume gives an elaborate understanding of the diverse changes, conflicts, emotional turmoil and identity crises that adolescent children go through and how parents and teachers can help them to handle this transitional stage.

This book will be of interest to psychologists, parents, students and teachers of psychology and scholars of child development, as well as professionals involved in working with children and adolescents, such as teachers, counsellors, doctors, nurses and social workers.

Veena Nandagiri has an MA degree in Counselling Psychology from Bombay University (Gold Medal – First Rank). She obtained her undergraduate degree from St. Xavier's College, Bombay. She has over 20 years of teaching experience and six years of counselling experience with school and college students in Mumbai and Mangalore. Ms. Veena Nandagiri has published articles in leading newspapers such as *The Hindu* and *Deccan Herald*, and in national and international journals. She has presented papers at international conferences and given talks on All India Radio, Mangalore. She has authored a book titled *Parenting – More Than 150 Tips* published in 2004.

Child-Adolescent Behaviour
A Psychological Perspective

Veena Nandagiri

LONDON AND NEW YORK

First published 2026
by Routledge
4 Park Square, Milton Park, Abingdon, Oxon OX14 4RN

and by Routledge
605 Third Avenue, New York, NY 10158

Routledge is an imprint of the Taylor & Francis Group, an informa business

© 2026 Veena Nandagiri

The right of Veena Nandagiri to be identified as author of this work has been asserted in accordance with sections 77 and 78 of the Copyright, Designs and Patents Act 1988.

All rights reserved. No part of this book may be reprinted or reproduced or utilised in any form or by any electronic, mechanical, or other means, now known or hereafter invented, including photocopying and recording, or in any information storage or retrieval system, without permission in writing from the publishers.

Trademark notice: Product or corporate names may be trademarks or registered trademarks, and are used only for identification and explanation without intent to infringe.

British Library Cataloguing-in-Publication Data
A catalogue record for this book is available from the British Library

ISBN: 978-1-032-40757-9 (hbk)
ISBN: 978-1-032-44616-5 (pbk)
ISBN: 978-1-003-37307-0 (ebk)

DOI: 10.4324/9781003373070

Typeset in Times New Roman
by Deanta Global Publishing Services, Chennai, India

I humbly dedicate this book to my loving mother Shanta, who, true to her name was an epitome of calmness and patience.

Contents

	Preface	*viii*
	Acknowledgements	*ix*
1	Family atmosphere and the child's personality	1
2	Influence of birth order on personality	13
3	Environmental factors influencing the child's development	20
4	Disciplining the child	36
5	Development of children's ambitions and aspirations	47
6	Developing the child's creativity	58
7	Learning disabilities in children	67
8	Behavioural/emotional disorders in children	80
9	Adolescence – a crucial period	99
	References	*111*
	Index	*126*

Preface

We are living in a fast changing world. The structure of the family is also changing and this affects the behaviour of children and adolescents to a great extent. So true is the saying by John C. Maxwell, "Change is inevitable, growth is optional". This book provides information about various factors that influence a child's behaviour and personality. Parents are the first social group and support system for a child and influence the child's growth, development and well-being in the most formative years. The child's parents, their family atmosphere and socio-cultural environment play a significant role in shaping the child's values and beliefs, self-concept and self-confidence, ambitions and goals, temperament and personality and consequently their behaviour in various situations. Included in this book are important theories and concepts of psychology, perspectives and views of psychologists and results of research studies on important topics like the pros and cons of discipline techniques and parenting styles, ways in which parents can foster the child's achievement and creativity, etc. The signs and interventions for some common learning disabilities and behavioural and emotional disorders in children are also explained. This book may interest and be useful to psychologists, parents, students and teachers of psychology, scholars of child development as well as professionals involved in working with children and adolescents such as teachers, counsellors, doctors, nurses and social workers. The list of references that are included can be used by students and teachers of psychology to explore new ideas for research, or to get more information on the topic.

Veena Nandagiri

Acknowledgements

Writing this book was a stimulating learning experience for me, a journey with its own challenges! However, every step towards its completion helped in my personal growth and shaped the final work. I am grateful to my husband, Professor Lakshman Nandagiri, for the continuous encouragement and guidance given to me while writing this book. I thank my son, Dr Ashwin, and daughter, Aarti, for the help rendered in preparing the manuscript and for their support. I am thankful to my parents, Professor N.S. Vasudeva Rao and Shanta Rao, for their unconditional love and appreciation. I acknowledge gratefully the help provided by Dr Mallikarjun Angadi, Librarian, NITK Surathkal (India), in the publication of this book. I thank Routledge (Taylor & Francis Group) for publishing the book. My experiences and interactions with students while teaching and providing counselling, my interactions with my children and parents and my upbringing and family atmosphere motivated me to write this book and I am indebted to them.

1 Family atmosphere and the child's personality

Chapter outline

- Personality
  - Definition
  - Factors influencing personality
  - Self-concept
- Importance of family
  - Family atmosphere
  - Needs
    - Maslow's hierarchy of needs
- Factors in the family influencing the child
- Steps to nurture a child's all-round development

Personality

Definition

Personality is the total quality of a person's behaviour as is shown in their habits of thinking, feeling and acting and attitudes, beliefs, values, interests, traits, self-concept, outward appearance and personal philosophy of life. According to Lindgren (1973), "personality refers to the relatively enduring and consistent aspects of our behaviour that cause us to resemble others in some ways and to be unique in other ways". He further states that personality includes the concepts of character (the kind of behaviour that is characteristic of an individual in key situations) and temperament (the individual's emotional tendencies). Both influence the way we interact with others and the kind of attitudes we develop towards ourselves and others.

According to Allport (1961), "personality is the dynamic organization within the individual of those psycho-physical systems that determine his unique adjustment to the environment". According to Allport,

> traits are the basic units of personality. A trait is a predisposition to respond and react in the same or similar manner to stimuli in the environment.

DOI: 10.4324/9781003373070-1

2 *Child-adolescent behaviour*

Traits have three properties: frequency, intensity, and range of situations. For example, a very submissive person would frequently be very submissive over a wide range of situations.

Traits explain the consistency of a person's behaviour; recognizing the importance of the situation is necessary to explain the variability of the behaviour. Allport put forward the concept of "proprium". It includes many aspects of the self (bodily self, self-identity, self-esteem) that the person seeks to organize into an integrated unified whole. Allport states that "Personality is many things in one – a unitas multiplex".

Pervin (1980) stated that "personality represents those characteristics of the person or of people generally that account for consistent patterns of response to situations".

According to the American Psychological Association (APA) *Dictionary of Psychology* (VandenBos, 2015),

Personality is the enduring configuration of characteristics and behaviour that comprises an individual's unique adjustment to life, including major traits, interests, drives, values, self-concept, abilities and emotional patterns. Personality helps determine behaviour. It is generally viewed as a complex dynamic integration or totality shaped by many forces, including hereditary and constitutional tendencies; physical maturation; early training; identification with significant individuals and groups; culturally conditioned values and roles; and critical experiences and relationships.

Factors influencing personality

According to Lindgren (1973), some aspects of a person's personality, that is his/her temperament, are biologically determined, but most aspects consist of learned behaviour patterns. As we play more significant roles in our lives, we learn ways of perceiving ourselves and our environment. These perceptual styles become aspects of our personality. "The roles that we learn also identify and define 'who we are' and constitute a major dimension of personality".

According to Coleman (1981),

The basic sources of personality development are heredity and environment. Heredity provides potentialities for development and behaviour typical of the species and is also an important source of individual differences. The person's physical and sociocultural environment also influences his personality development. Different environments foster different personality characteristics. Different subgroups within a general sociocultural environment such as family, sex, age, social class, occupational and religious groups also foster beliefs and norms of their own, largely by means of social roles that their members learn to adopt. There are expected

Family and the child's personality 3

role behaviours and role demands for a student, teacher, priest, nurse and persons occupying other specific positions. These role expectations also influence personality development. No two individuals grow in the same environment. Thus a person's sociocultural environment is the source of differences and commonalities in personality development. A person's genetic inheritance interacts with environmental factors and a self-structure emerges. This becomes an important influence in shaping the person's further development and behaviour.

Two important factors that influence a child's personality development and also make them unique are hereditary factors (genetic inheritance) and environmental factors.

The *hereditary* factors that influence a child's personality include physique, physical appearance, physical disability, intelligence level, nature of glandular functioning and physiological conditions of the body. The physique and physical appearance of the person influences their self-perception, others' reactions towards them and, consequently, personality development. For instance, a person who is very short may feel shy. Glandular imbalance, such as excess insulin secreted by the pancreas, may make the person anxious and tired. The physiological conditions of a person's body brought about by drugs, disease, poor physical health or physical disability, toxins or infections influence a person's behaviour and personality.

The *environmental* factors that influence personality development include:

* The child's parents, family members, home atmosphere and economic condition of the family.
* The school, teachers, teaching method, personality and attitude of teachers, type of discipline, richness of curriculum and the curricular and extra-curricular activities.
* The child's friends, neighbours, peer group, social roles, political conditions, mass media, social media and culture. Culture refers to beliefs, customs, norms and moral values that are passed down from generation to generation.

According to Coleman (1981),

our genetic environment provides our potentialities for both biological and psychological development, but the shaping of these potentialities – in terms of perceiving, thinking, feeling and acting – depends heavily on our physical and sociocultural environment. Heredity/our genetic inheritance influences the development of some traits more than others. Its influence is more noticeable in physical features, such as eye colour and physique,

4   *Child-adolescent behaviour*

and also in "primary reaction tendencies" like activity level, sensitivity to stimuli, and adaptability.

A person's heredity and environment jointly shape their abilities, psychological characteristics, intelligence, physical and mental health and personality. The person's inheritance provides potentialities for behaviour. The person's environment determines whether these potentialitites will be realized to the fullest or not.

Self-concept

The self-concept is an important dimension of a person's personality and embodies the answer to the question "who am I?" It is the descriptive component of one's self, for example, "I believe that I am fast runner". According to Jersild et al. (1975),

> The *self* as it finally evolves is made up of all that goes into a person's experiences of his individual existence. It is a person's inner world. It is a composite of a person's thoughts and feelings, strivings and hopes, fears and fantasies, his view of what he is, what he has been, what he might become and his attitudes pertaining to his worth.

According to Lindgren (1973),

> we play important roles in our life. As a result, we learn more about "who we are". This is a major dimension of our personality. The self-concept refers to the attitudes we have towards our self and conceptions of our self. It is affected by the roles we play and affects the roles as well.

According to Crow and Crow (1962), the environmental factors within and outside the family that influence the child's developing self-concept are as follows:

1. Within the home:
   - Parent's expectations.
   - Family personal problems.
   - Family economic level.
   - Attitude of and towards family members.
   - Religious affiliation.
2. Outside the home:
   - School demands.
   - School opportunities.
   - Opinion of peers.

Family and the child's personality 5

- Attitude towards peers.
- Impact of mass media.
- Physical state of the child.
- Biological maturation (early, average, late).

According to Rathus and Nevid (2002), a person's self-concept is his/her impression or concept of himself/herself. It includes his/her own listing of personal traits like fairness, sociability, etc., which he considers important and is his evaluation of how he rates himself according to these traits. And this influences whether the person likes himself and how much he likes himself. The person's self-concept is multifaceted. It includes his/her (a) self-evaluation (b) sense of personal worth/self-esteem (c) sense of who and what he would like to be/ideal self (d) sense of competence to meet his goals/self-efficacy.

Self-esteem refers to a person's self-perceived competence, for example "I feel good that I am a fast runner". According to Lindgren (1973),

> self-esteem is the amount of value we ascribe to our self and is based on the esteem others have for us. It develops in childhood and is fostered by positive, accepting and satisfying relationships with parents. Persons with high levels of self-esteem are likely to rate high on independence.

A person's self-esteem refers to their self-respect and depends on factors like social approval, competence and discrepancy between the way a person sees themself and who they think they ought to be (Rathus and Nevid, 2002). According to Robins et al. (2001), self-esteem is positively correlated with the person's psychological and physical health. Paul and Brier (2001) found that high self-esteem helped first-year students to handle the stresses of the transition to college, such as missing their high school friends.

Orth et al. (2008) found that low self-esteem in a child may contribute to the child having an emotional disability like depression in adolescence and/or young adulthood. They suggest that emotional reactions like depression can be prevented or reduced by increasing the child's self-esteem.

Ideal self: According to Rathus and Nevid (2002), a person's concept of what they "should be" or "ought to be" is called the self-ideal or ideal-self. The closer the person's self-description is to the ideal self, the higher the person's self-esteem will be. They state that a student with average performance may have higher self-esteem than a student with very good performance. This may be because the former may not value scholarship and high marks, whereas the latter may be a perfectionist and so will not be happy even with good achievements, so their self-esteem will be lower.

Importance of family

The family is the first and the most influential factor in the life of any individual. According to Rogers (1951),

6   *Child-adolescent behaviour*

a very important and the first aspect of self-experience of a child is that he/she is loved by his/her parents. He perceives himself as lovable and worthy of love and develops affection to his parents. He feels satisfied and this is an important element of the structure of the self as it begins to form. Everyone has within himself the potentiality for growth in positive directions. When the individual is placed in a permissive, accepting environment, the process of self-actualization occurs.

Miller (1971) describes the child–parent relationship by saying that

> for a child the family is the primary social unit. The parents, within this family structure, act as socializing agents in providing values and goals from which the child develops various patterns of behaviour. Such behavioural patterns form the basis for interaction with others. These behaviour patterns elicit reactions in the form of verbal and/or non-verbal responses from these significant others. These responses serve as indicators to the child of who he is and how others feel about him. If the child gets more positive responses he develops a favourable concept of self and this results in self-actualization. The more negative the attitudes and feelings expressed through the responses of others, the more incongruent is the state of the individual and the less likely are his chances of attaining self-actualization.

Family atmosphere

A healthy family atmosphere is very important because the family provides the child with emotional security in their formative years. Within the family, the attitude of the parents towards the child, adequate satisfaction of the child's needs, an atmosphere of mutual understanding between family members and love, affection and attention from parents will help the child to develop self-respect and self-confidence. According to the "emotional security theory" by Cummings and Davies (1996),

> emotional security is a state of calmness wherein the person does not get overwhelmed by negative emotions, that is, he/she has good self-control. Emotional security can be enhanced or undermined by the type and quality of family relations. If there is too much disagreement between parents, it threatens the child's sense of security. If parents use hostile strategies to communicate with each other, children feel worried and insecure and they may show sleep disturbances, health problems like stomach ache or aggressive behaviour. Siblings may become overinvolved or overprotective of each other or distant and disengaged with each other. But if marital disagreement is mild or moderate, with more compromise, children enjoy

Family and the child's personality 7

emotional security, self-esteem, have better social skills, develop better relationships with parents and have fewer psychological problems.

According to Rathus and Nevid (2002),

The beginning of a child's self-esteem depends on parents' love and approval. If children are cherished by their parents, they consider themselves worthy of love and are likely to learn to love and accept themselves. If parents are involved with their children's activities, it communicates worthiness. If parents encourage their child to develop competence, it contributes to their self-esteem and is an expression of their love and caring.

Coopersmith (1967) studied the relation between different patterns of parent–child interaction and the development of self-esteem in pre-adolescent children. Coopersmith found that the parents of children with high self-esteem set rules and guided their children firmly but carefully and used rewards. Details of "the effects of rewards, punishment and discipline techniques" are provided in Chapter 4 of this book.

Needs

A child's physical needs of food, water, etc., and psychological needs such as the need for recognition, affection, etc., should be satisfied by the family. A need is a necessity of life and directs a person's activity towards a goal. It becomes a motivating force in human activities. Psychological needs are related to the mental health and development of the self in the child and must be satisfied by parents for the child's healthy socio-emotional development. "A psychological need is a psychological nutrient that is essential for individuals' adjustment, integrity and growth" (Ryan and Deci, 2000).

Maslow's hierarchy of needs

Maslow's hierarchy of needs is a well-known and widely accepted motivational theory in psychology. He proposed a *five-stage model of human needs* that is arranged in a *hierarchy of prepotency*. It was published by Abraham Maslow in 1943 in his paper titled "A theory of human motivation" and suggests that a person has to fulfil basic needs first, before moving on to more advanced needs. When the most prepotent goal is realized, the next higher need emerges. Thus, man is a perpetually wanting animal. This framework is widely used to understand human motivation and personal development. The needs at the lower levels of the hierarchy must be satisfied before individuals can attend to needs higher up. From the bottom of the *hierarchy* upwards, the needs are as follows:

8 Child-adolescent behaviour

1. Physiological needs (the need for food, water, shelter).
2. Safety needs (the need to feel safe and secure from physical threat and harsh weather and being cared for during illness).
3. Love and belonging needs (the need for affectionate relationships with family and friends).
4. Esteem needs (the need for self-respect and respect from others. Self-respect includes the desire for competence and achievement. Respect from others includes the desire for attention, recognition and acceptance from others).
5. Self-actualization (the desire for personal growth, self-fulfilment and realizing one's full potential). Maslow's theory suggests that individuals strive to fulfil these needs in a hierarchical sequence, with higher-level needs becoming active once lower-level ones are met.

Maslow postulates that esteem needs may be divided into two categories. First, self-esteem, that is, the desire for strength, competence and confidence in front of others, and it produces adequacy and usefulness when satisfied. Secondly, respect from others involves the need to be recognized, respected and appreciated by others. Individuals sometimes participate in activities to gain recognition. Maslow further states that the healthiest self-esteem needs are based on respect from others, that is, deserved rather than unwarranted respect, such as one that comes with extreme fame. A lack of self-esteem and missing respect from others can produce feelings of inferiority. According to Maslow, this need is most important for children and adolescents to create a sense of real self-esteem and dignity.

Maslow calls the first four levels "deficiency needs" and the highest level the "growth/being needs". If the deficit needs are not realized, this can have physical and psychological consequences for the individual. As a person fulfils their growth needs, their motivation increases and also their desire to become better increases.

Family factors that influence the child

The factors within the family influencing the child's mental health, self-esteem and adjustment are:

- *The attitude of parents towards the child.* Parents must not overprotect their children, reject them nor be permissive. They must give them adequate love, affection and attention, be understanding and encourage them to become independent.

  Overprotection means parents exhibit an exaggerated amount of concern for their children, do everything for them and shield them from difficulties. If a child is overprotected they may seek love, admiration

Family and the child's personality 9

and help from others even after they grow up. The following are some reasons why parents may become overprotective.

- If the child is sick right from birth, this necessitates great physical care. But even after the child has recovered, this parental attitude may be maintained, so much so that it leads to overprotection.
- If a child is unwanted by their parents for some reason, the parents may sometimes develop negative feelings and attitudes towards their child. The parent may become overprotective to mask this feeling.
- Parents may not want their child to grow up and assert independence and so they may become overprotective.

Mathijs et al. (2023) found that there is a significant association between overprotective parenting and social anxiety symptoms in the adolescent. The reason for this is that overprotective parenting does not give the child a chance to develop their emotional regulation skills and this can make the child show emotional reactions like social anxiety. To help children develop emotional regulation skills and avoid overprotection, parents should do the following:

- Let their child face difficult situations and experience negative emotions.
- Help the child to understand their own emotions and let them practise emotional regulation strategies.
- Allow the child autonomy to make their own decisions whenever possible.
- Model coping skills and role-play difficult situations for the child.

Another faulty attitude that parents may adopt towards their child is that of rejection. *Rejection* means being strict with children, punishing them and not showering love on them. Parents may develop this attitude due to one of these reasons:

- It may be due to the unwelcome birth of the child.
- It may be because the child is not of the gender that the parents desired.
- A father may reject their child if the mother died in childbirth.

Cowell et al. (2015) found that children who were not treated well during infancy showed poorer inhibitory control and working memory performance than children who were treated well.

Permissiveness means giving children complete freedom. If parents are permissive, children may not learn self-control and self-discipline. Children are more secure, happy and prepared to deal with life when parents provide direction and encourage the child to behave in accordance with rules.

- *An unsatisfactory relationship between the parents.* According to the emotional security theory of Cummings and Davies (1996), too much conflict and hostility between parents is an environmental stressor

10 *Child-adolescent behaviour*

and comes in the way of the child's adjustment even in later life and can affect their confidence. Children may show emotional reactions like fear, anger, sadness, be inattentive in school and have academic problems.

Children from homes with high levels of conflict had more physical disabilities, health and social problems and showed reactions such as depression, loneliness, substance dependency and emotional reactivity (Repetti et al., 2002).

- *Single parent home.* If children grow up with only one parent in the home, they get affection/attention and care from only one parent and this influences the child's behaviour and adjustment. According to the study by Pearson et al. (1994), teachers rated fourth-grade children who lived with their mother alone as showing more aggressive behaviour than children who lived with both parents.

- *Loss in the family.* Some types of loss/difficult circumstances in the home adversely affect the growing child's behaviour and learning, for example, experiencing domestic violence at home, having parents who have a drug/alcohol problem or are receiving mental health treatment. Children may not be able to concentrate on studies or may not follow rules, may become quiet or show emotional reactions like anxiety. Copeland et al. (2007) studied children between 9 and 16 years of age. They found that children who experienced unpleasant events or difficulties had more chances of developing anxiety and depressive disorders. Behere et al. (2017) studied children who were admitted to inpatient psychiatric units and found that 89 per cent of the children who were admitted had some disruption in their family structure.

- *The principles, values and behaviour of parents.* Children learn a lot by observing, imitating and identifying with parents according to social learning theory (Bandura, 1977). Identification means the child thinks, acts and feels like the person they select as a model as they admire that person. The person may be a parent, teacher, sibling, peer or a popular hero. The more affection the child has for a parent, the more the child will identify with them, so parents must display virtues and behaviours that they want their child to imbibe.

  According to Cummings and Kouros (2008), mild conflict between parents does not affect the child's security as children often learn how to sort out their differences by observing their parents. They also learn social skills and show fewer adjustment problems.

- *Exposure to violence in the school/at home/on media.* If the teacher resorts to corporal punishment with the students, it conveys the message to them that it is legitimate to hit someone if they make a mistake, so the child may beat their classmate if they feel they have been hurt by the

Family and the child's personality 11

classmate or if the classmate made a mistake. Children who are exposed to violence at home or see it in movies or TV programmes may mimic violent behaviour. Students who have been bullied or teased by classmates or senior students may show aggressive behaviour.

Bandura et al. (1961) investigated whether (1) children of three to six years would learn aggressive reactions by observing a model behaving aggressively towards a doll and (2) whether they would reproduce this behaviour in the absence of the model. They found that children exposed to aggressive models imitated their exact behaviour. They were significantly more aggressive than children in other groups who were not exposed to aggressive models. Boys imitated more physically aggressive acts. This study has important implications for the effects that exposure to violence in media can have on a child.

- *The position of the child in the family.* The child's ordinal position affects their personality, self-concept and parent–child interaction. Details of "the influence of the ordinal position on the behaviour of children" are provided in Chapter 2 of this book.
- *Relations such as grandparents, uncles and aunts.* It is a common occurrence in a family with parents and grandparents that parents and grandparents differ in the way they discipline the child. Consequently, the child feels confused and does not know whom to follow, so, parents and grandparents must be in agreement regarding discipline.

Steps to nurture a child's all-round development

Parents should aim to help their child to be physically fit, mentally alert, emotionally stable, socially acceptable and morally upright, that is, to develop an integrated and well-balanced personality. To become good architects of the child's all-round personality development they can do the following:

- They must cater to the child's *physical development* by giving good and nutritious food and encouraging them to participate in sports and games. Play promotes physical, motor, social, emotional and cognitive development.
- Parents must foster the child's *intellectual development* by cultivating an interest in learning in the child by telling them stories. They must develop the child's skills of reading good books, writing, drawing, painting and other extra-curricular activities.
- Parents must lay the foundation for the child's *character development* by cultivating good manners, conduct and ethical values in the child.
- As children grow up, parents must express *faith* in them and *confidence* in their growing independence. Parents must invite the participation of

12 *Child-adolescent behaviour*

children in planning group activities and in making decisions about family affairs.

- Parents must help their child to *deal with stress*. Some common causes of stress in children are not getting sufficient love and attention from parents, sibling rivalry, having teachers who show partiality, not being able to get along with school mates and too much academic pressure.

2 Influence of birth order on personality

Chapter Outline

- Birth order and personality
- The only child versus a child with siblings
  - Advantages of being an only child
  - Disadvantages of being an only child
  - Advantages of having siblings
  - Disadvantages of having siblings
- Sibling rivalry
  - Causes
  - Steps to reduce sibling rivalry

Birth order and personality

Birth order is the rank of siblings by age and has an effect on a person's personality. According to the APA *Dictionary of Psychology* (VandenBos, 2015) "birth order is the ordinal position of the child in the family (first-born, second-born, youngest, etc.)". Adler (1928), an Austrian psychoanalyst, was one of the first theorists to suggest that birth order influences personality and can leave an indelible impression on an individual's style of life, which is one's habitual way of dealing with tasks of friendship, love and work. According to Adler, first-borns are "dethroned" when a second child comes along and this may have a lasting influence on them. Younger and older children may be pampered, which can also affect their later personalities. Additional birth order factors that should be considered are the spacing in years between siblings, the total number of children and the changing circumstances of parents over time. Adler (1964) noted the importance of understanding the "Family Constellation".

It is a common fallacy to imagine that children of the same family are formed in the same environment. Of course there is much which is same

DOI: 10.4324/9781003373070-2

14 *Child-adolescent behaviour*

for all in the same home, but the psychic situation of each child is individual and differs from that of others because of the order of their succession.

Paulhus et al. (1999) found that first-borns scored higher on conservatism, conscientiousness and achievement orientation. Later-born children scored higher on rebelliousness, openness and aggression. Only children share many characteristics with first-born children including being conscientious and parent-oriented.

Sulloway (1996) held that birth order has powerful effects on a person's personality. It affects the big five personality traits – openness, conscientiousness, extroversion, agreeableness and neuroticism. First-borns who are physically superior to their siblings at a young age, tend to be socially dominant, less agreeable, more conservative and less open to new ideas. They conform to parental values and societal expectations. Later-born children are more likely to rebel against their parents and authority. They try to develop an array of strategies to distinguish themselves and they tend to be more creative, rebellious and sympathetic to underdogs. First-born children are secure with their place in the family and are expected to be mature so they often grow up to be intellectual, responsible and conformist. Younger siblings work harder to get their parents' attention, take more risks and become creative rebels. Middle children score higher in agreeableness than both their older and younger siblings.

Sulloway (1998) said that first-born children are bigger in size and have more status as they are older than their siblings. They use some methods against their younger brothers and sisters like hitting them. Each child carves out a distinct niche for themself in the family. First-borns occupy the niche of a surrogate parent, i.e., they help their parents in taking care of their younger siblings. So, they not only identify more with their parents, but they also follow their values, are more hard-working and try to do well in academics. The younger children try to see if they can compete in a niche occupied by their elder sibling. If they cannot, they try to fare well in some other field where they need not compete with the elder sibling. So, they are often more creative than the eldest child. Only children do not have siblings with whom to interact and hence do not experience sibling rivalry. They do not have to compete or prove themselves to an older or younger sibling. So, they are "free to occupy any niche they wish to in childhood" and their behaviour, interests and traits are not easy to predict. Sulloway's work shows the profound influence that a person's family has on the personalities of children. Sibling competition affects individual development within the family.

Leman (1982) held that birth order has a powerful influence on the way people interact with others, whether at home or outside. He details a person's personality type based on a person's birth order. First-born people are leaders and want approval from those in charge. They can be aggressive. Middle children want to be the opposite of their older siblings and often feel they are

Influence of birth order on personality 15

ignored in favour of their older and younger siblings. They can be secretive. Last-born children are social and also manipulative. Leman considered the only-child type to be a form of the first-born family type.

Yang et al. (2017) found that only children scored higher in flexibility (a dimension of creativity) and lower on agreeableness (a personality trait) than children with siblings.

According to Trent and Spitze (2011), there are three theoretical arguments for why children with siblings differ from only children in terms of social activities.

- According to the "resource dilution" model, if there are more children in a household, fewer resources are available to any child. Only children benefit from their parents' undivided attention in the education field and in the development of social skills.
- According to the "siblings as resources model" siblings are social capital. Only children have no sibling interaction at home and hence do not have the benefit of important social learning experiences.
- The "only child uniqueness" argument suggests that the at-home experiences of the only child are similar to the first-born and a little like the last born so it is unique. As a result, only children master skills related to solitary pursuits.

Oliva and Arranz (2005) analyzed sibling relationships during adolescence and found gender-based differences. When girls had a good relationship with their siblings, they also had a good relationship with their parents and peers. They had higher self-esteem and satisfaction with life. Their study found no relation with family or other personal variables for boys.

The only child versus a child with siblings

Advantages of being an only child

- According to Downey (2001), only children perform better on tests of cognitive skills than children with siblings because they get attention from both parents. Downey (2001) uses the "Resource Dilution Model" to explain this – siblings reduce the amount of time, attention, energy and financial resources that any one child can receive from parents. So, the fewer, the better.
- Only children use adult language as they interact with parents most of the time. According to Bhattacharya and Biswas (2013), since they spend most of their time with adults, they are mature and have subtle control over their emotions.

16 *Child-adolescent behaviour*

Disadvantages of being an only child

- An only child has to bear the pressures of expectations of both parents and this may cause emotional stress and strain.
- An only child might be lonely after their parents die because they will have no siblings.
- An only child does not have to share things with siblings and so may sometimes find it more challenging to share or adjust with others. Downey and Condron (2004) state that kindergarten teachers found that only children have less self-control, poorer interpersonal skills and more problem behaviours than those with even one sibling. Siblings serve as resources and children tend to negotiate peer relationships better if they grow up with siblings.
- According to the "siblings as resources model" siblings are social capital. Only children have no sibling interaction at home and hence do not have the benefit of important social learning experience (Trent and Spitze, 2011).

Advantages of having siblings

- Siblings can be a source of emotional security for each other. This means that in confusing and stressful situations, they can offer support and advice. Codes of loyalty, helpfulness and protection may be strong between brothers and sisters. Merry et al. (2020) hold that sibling relationships involve both positive and negative emotions. They provide children a chance to resolve conflicts at home. This helps them interact and form relationships with peers, understand other people's emotions or viewpoints and control their own emotions.
- There are some childhood secrets that can only be shared among siblings. Younger siblings benefit from older siblings, such as in education and relationships in social life. They may sometimes make better decisions by observing their older siblings' behaviour or mistakes. Merry et al. (2020) studied how growing up with siblings influences a child's ability to get along with peers and eventually develop long-term meaningful relationships. They found that siblings help in the development of social skills.
- Many times parents do not understand their child's viewpoint due to the generation gap. Brothers and sisters could prove dependable in such cases. Downey and Condron (2004) found that during the stage of early adulthood, siblings provide psychological support to each other and thus help to maintain psychological well-being.
- After the parents die, siblings may offer support.

Influence of birth order on personality 17

Disadvantages of having siblings

- When children are young, they have to share toys, things and their parents' attention with siblings. The psychologist, Adler (1928), called this "dethronement". The first child is like a prince/princess to the parents. Other children dethrone the first child by taking away the parents' affection and attention. The effects of dethronement or lack of it (as in the case of only children) determine personality traits such as children's sense of responsibility, their attitudes towards authority, their self-esteem and achievement motivation.
- After they grow up, there may be problems of inheritance among siblings.
- Many-a-times, parents make comparisons between children and favour one child over the other. This *parental favouritism* can manifest in different ways such as displaying more affection or spending more time with one child, giving more privileges/praise to the favoured child or being less strict or more lenient with the favoured child. Parental favouritism has a negative impact on children's mental health and can lead to emotional/behavioural problems in them. If a child feels that their sibling is being favoured or if the parents label one child as more beautiful or smarter than the other, it hurts their self-esteem. They may show emotional reactions like depression or aggressive behaviour. It can strain the relationship between siblings. The child who is put down feels unloved and may have personality and adjustment problems.
- People do not forget that they were disfavoured in childhood by their parents and this can have an effect on their self-esteem and relationship with the favoured sibling, even in adulthood.

Sibling rivalry

According to the *APA Dictionary of Psychology* (VandenBos, 2015) "sibling rivalry refers to the competition among siblings for the attention, affection or approval of one or both parents or for other recognition or rewards, such as in sports or academics". Rivalry or conflict between siblings is common, regardless of the age difference between siblings. When a new baby is born, the seeds of sibling rivalry are sown because the elder sibling sees the younger one as a potential rival for parental attention. Further, the elder child also has to share things, toys and their room with the new sibling.

Causes

Factors that may cause rivalry between siblings include:

- Natural evolution. As children grow, they develop individual needs and personalities. They may differ in ideas, attitude and temperament and

18 *Child-adolescent behaviour*

this may be the cause of conflict between them. One child may be so possessive about their belongings that they may find it difficult to accept their sibling using those things. The other child may have such an innate sense of sharing that they are angry that the elder one does not share things with them.

- "You love them more". Many children grow up with the conviction that the other child is more important to the parents and loved more than them. This may make them point out the mistakes of the other child. Sometimes parents may give more attention to one child either because they have an emotional problem/physical disability/learning disability or an exceptional talent in some field. This may be difficult and stressful to handle for the other sibling. Parents must explain the cause of the unequal treatment to the disfavoured child so as to reduce the negative consequences.
- Suitor et al. (2009) found that perceived maternal favouritism affects sibling relationships not only in childhood but also in adulthood. Adults recollect their mother's favouritism towards their siblings in their childhood years. This influences their relationships with siblings in adulthood. Suitor et al. also found that when mothers did not display favouritism to any child in the family, the siblings were very close to each other. Another finding was that sisters reported closer relationships than their brothers.
- Differences in temperament. As children differ in temperament from one another, an independent child may fight with the sibling who is always turning to their parents for attention. However, a child with a laid-back attitude may find a focused sibling's behaviour unacceptable.
- Parental behaviour. Children learn a lot by observation and imitation. Those who see their parents treat each other with respect and a strong sense of fair play will learn acceptable behaviour from them (Cummings and Kouros, 2008). Conflict between parents may precipitate and aggravate sibling rivalry. It affects sibling relationships, causing them to become distant and disengaged with each other or overly involved and overprotective of each other (Cummings and Davies, 1996).

Steps to reduce sibling rivalry

- Parents should not make comparisons between their children or point out one child's shortcomings in comparison with their siblings as this will cause unpleasant feelings. The parents must accept the fact that each child is unique.
- Parents must encourage each child to develop their own special skills and avoid putting a personality stamp on their child. If children are handled in this way they will be supportive of each other.
- Parents must guard against favouritism and be as fair as possible.

Influence of birth order on personality 19

- If children are arguing or fighting with each other, parents should let them sort out their differences themselves. Only if the situation gets out of control should they step in and initiate negotiations.
- Parents must understand that sibling rivalry is a means by which, on the way to adulthood, children learn the rules of engagement, negotiation, compromise and resolution. According to Downey (2001), children learn the intricacies of socializing better through their siblings. Sibling rivalry ensuing from competing for resources at home and for academic, financial and emotional elements from parents often acts as a precursor for coping in later life. The idea of what resources to share, where to compete, etc., is obtained in a non-formal environment in the home through siblings, and this teaches the child to make adjustments.

3 Environmental factors influencing the child's development

Chapter outline

- Introduction
- Games/play and the child
  - Introduction
  - Stages of play
  - Different types of play
  - The role of play in the child's development
  - Theories of play
- Friends and the child
  - Introduction
  - Factors influencing friendship formation
  - Sullivan's theory of friendship
  - The role of friends in the child's development
- The impact of print media on the child
- The impact of television on the child
- The influence of social media and the internet on the child
- Daydreaming/mind-wandering and the child
  - Introduction
  - Benefits of daydreaming
  - Drawbacks of daydreaming
  - Types of daydream

Introduction

Games, friends, print media, internet, social media and daydreams are some important environmental factors that influence a child's behaviour, development and adjustment. Play is the principal means of learning in early childhood. Children must be encouraged to play both indoor and outdoor games because it helps in the all-round development of their personality. Children must have friends of their own age to play with because friends serve many important functions. Children love to read and hear stories. Parents must encourage their child's reading interests and also tell them stories because

DOI: 10.4324/9781003373070-3

Environment and the child's development 21

stories help the child's intellectual and moral growth. Children and adolescents spend time daydreaming. Daydreams are fantasies that children have during the day, when they are awake. Daydreaming is a natural and useful pastime if kept within bounds. Children are now spending time using social media and the internet. It has advantages but too much use of social media is not good for the child.

Games/play and the child

Introduction

Playing games has an important role in a child's life as it helps in their adjustment and overall development. Play is so important for a child's optimal development that the United Nations High Commission for Human Rights has recognized it as a right of every child. It is an enjoyable activity for young children that is usually spontaneous. It offers parents a wonderful opportunity to engage with children, understand their views and frustrations and build strong relations with them (Tamis-Le-Monda et al., 2004).

Children engage in play out of interest and there is no time-bound goal for them to achieve. Play influences a child's physical, emotional, social and cognitive development and helps them to express their creativity (Ginsbury, 2007).

Children learn to manage their feelings, communicate with others, to reason and imagine and take risks. They act out adult roles of the society in which they live, such as teacher–student or parent–child interactions (Pelligrini and Smith, 1998).

Stages of play

There are six stages of play during early childhood and they help in the child's development. They involve exploring, being creative, learning social skills and having fun (Anderson-Mcnamee and Bailey, 2010). The stages are as follows:

- *Unoccupied play.* (Birth to three months) The baby moves their arms, legs, hands and feet. They are learning about how the body moves.
- *Solitary play.* (Birth to two years) The child is not interested in playing with others and likes to play alone. It is independent play.
- *Spectator behaviour/onlooker behaviour.* (Two years) Children like to watch other children playing but do not play with them. They learn the rules of the game and about human interactions and this helps the child to build skills and gain confidence to engage in play.
- *Parallel play.* (Over two years) The child plays alongside or near others but not with them. Neither child influences the play of the other but they learn from each other.

22   Child-adolescent behaviour

- *Associative play*. (Three to five years) Children interact and communicate with each other but do not cooperate much. This is the first stage when they start building friendships and relationships. They learn language through communication. An example of associative play is children playing in a park doing different things.
- *Cooperative play*. (Over five years) The child likes to play with others and has an interest in both the play activity and other children involved in playing. Children learn social skills.

Different types of play

- *Motor/physical play*: Children run, jump and develop muscle skills.
- *Constructive play*: Children create things, for example, playing with sand, building blocks, drawing and painting. Children discover patterns, explore objects to find out what works and what does not work. They gain confidence and pride after accomplishment.
- *Expressive play*: Some types of play and play materials help children to express their feelings. Materials like paints, crayons, a drawing board or paper, sand, water, clay and sponges help them to experience different textures. Rhythm instruments and beanbags also help the child to express themself.

Role of play in the child's development

- Games help the child's *physical and motor development*. Outdoor games such as running, playing on the slide and swings, etc., provide children with a chance to exercise their growing muscles, develop hand-eye coordination, learn to balance and thus refine their motor skills. It increases the physical activity of children and this helps to reduce obesity (American Academy of Pediatrics, 2006). Games help children's physical development and they feel they can control their body. This gives them a feeling of satisfaction and confidence and contributes to their self-esteem. This does not happen when children watch television, use a computer or play video games for long periods of time, since the child is a passive recipient (Ginsbury, 2007). Playing vigorous games helps children to have a good appetite and get good sleep.
- Games help the child's *social development*. Play allows for social interactions and this helps in social–emotional learning (Smith, 1995). When children play with friends they learn to cooperate with others and some behaviours like:
  - to share, to take turns, to give the first turn to somebody else,to wait for their turn, to be humble about their skills and follow the rules of the game, to abide by the decision of the majority even if it is not to their personal liking, to be friendly and helpful, to lose cheerfully,

Environment and the child's development 23

to encourage a shy or timid player, to share scarce equipment and to be fair and honest, to comfort the one who has lost. Team games where children have to play together and pool in their efforts to win, to share material and experiences tend to generate cooperation. Play teaches children to experience others' points of view by working through conflicts about space, materials or rules positively. Games teach children how to compete with others, to face defeat and that they must strive hard to win. This mentally prepares them to take care of themselves in the competitive world when they grow up.

- Games/play help in the child's *emotional development* and to conquer their fears (Erickson, 1985). Games provide children with situations in which they can vent their feelings and get over their unpleasant feelings of hurt, anger, etc., by acting them out in games.

According to Piaget (1962), "pretend play" helps children to express feelings in the following ways:

- *Simplifying events* by creating an imaginary character, plot or setting to match their emotional state. For example, a child who is afraid of the dark might eliminate darkness or night from the play episode.
- *Compensating* for situations by adding forbidden acts to pretend play. For example, a child may eat ice cream or chocolate in play, whereas in reality this would not be permitted.
- *Controlling emotional expression* by repeatedly re-enacting unpleasant or frightening experiences. For example, a child might pretend to have an accident after seeing a real traffic accident on the highway.
- *Avoiding adverse consequences* by pretending that another character, real or imaginary, commits inappropriate acts and suffers the consequences. For example, children whose television viewing is monitored at home may pretend to allow the doll to watch television indiscriminately and then reprimand the "bad child" for unacceptable television viewing habits.
- Games help the child's *cognitive development*. In play, children develop concepts of causal relationships, the power to discriminate, to analyze, to reason, to make judgements, to synthesize, to count and to focus on the game. They learn new competencies that increase their confidence and resilience (Hurwitz, 2002). According to Bodrova and Leong (2005), dramatic or pretend play in early childhood can foster young children's cognitive and social development. Teachers can encourage such play in the classroom in which children create a pretend scenario and they interact with peers by creating specific roles and they follow some rules. Games help in the development of the child's imagination. In play, children sometimes imagine that they are someone else and they think, feel, work, act and behave like them.

24 *Child-adolescent behaviour*

- Games help in the development of the child's *creativity* as play allows a flexible situation. While playing, children handle, manipulate, explore and create new things with what is present around them such as clay, paper, waste material, etc. (Tsao, 2002). For instance, a string of empty matchboxes can be a train.
- Play *improves parent–child relationships* (Anderson-McNamee and Bailey, 2010). They can understand the child's temperament and views better and build lasting bonds with their child. Children feel happy and important when parents play with them and this increases their self-esteem. Playing with children can be a stress buster for overworked parents.

Theories of play

Based on a literature review by Verenikina et al. (2003), the following are some theories that explain the ways in which play helps in a child's development:

- *Psychoanalytic theories*. They hold that play helps a child as it decreases their anxiety aroused by stressful experiences. It provides the child with an acceptable way to express suppressed impulses and gives children a feeling of control over their world.
- *Cognitive theory*. Play strengthens the child's existing learning. It also helps the child to understand new concepts, solve problems and learn different skills.
- *Arousal modulation theory*. Play keeps the child engaged as it reduces feelings of uncertainty and increases interest by reducing boredom. It keeps the body at an optimal state of arousal.
- *The theory of self*. Play contributes to the child's sense of self, i.e., their "I" or identity and the child's social relations.
- *Socio-cultural theory*. Play fosters a child's conceptual or abstract thinking as the child uses their toys and other objects in symbolic ways. Play helps the child explore social roles and follow societal rules.

Friends and the child

Introduction

Friends play an important role in a person's life. According to the APA *Dictionary of Psychology* (VandenBos, 2015) "*Friendship* is a voluntary relationship between two or more people that is relatively long-lasting and in which those involved tend to be concerned with meeting the others' needs and interests as well as satisfying their own desires". Most people describe a friend based on mutuality and reciprocity, including the expectations that friends support one another and that give and take are at the foundation of

Environment and the child's development 25

the relationship (Bigelow, 1977). Friendships are often described as "horizontal" relationships because of the sense of equality that is at their core. Hartup and Stevens (1997) differentiate between the deep structure and surface structure of friendship. The deep structure that is the essence of friendship is "reciprocity". It remains the same across the lifespan. But the surface structure, that is, the "social exchange" or the actual interactions that occur between friends changes with age according to the developmental tasks connected with that period. According to Hartup and Stevens (1997), in young children, playing together and sharing defines friendship, but in adolescence, close intimate relationships define friendships. Some emotions shared by friends are affection, sympathy, empathy, mutual understanding, honesty, compassion, trust, altruism, enjoyment of each other's company and the ability to be oneself, to express one's feelings and make mistakes without fear of judgement from the friend. Having friends is correlated with a sense of well-being across the lifespan but the developmental outcome also depends on the identity of one's friends as well as the quality of one's relationships with them.

According to Rathus and Nevid (2002), at each developmental stage, friends satisfy some needs of the child. According to Berndt and Perry (1986), primary school children make friends with those who sit next to them in class or those who live next door. Their friends are those classmates with whom they have fun. For middle school or secondary school children, friends are those who have similar interests to their own. In adolescence, the child wants friends to share their experiences, feelings, etc., and the friend should not reveal the child's secrets or stories to others. In late adolescence and early adulthood, the child starts belonging to cliques and crowds. A clique is a small number of close friends who share confidences. A crowd is a large group of friends who share activities but are not very intimate with each other.

According to Bagwell and Schmidt (2011), friendships are voluntary, reciprocal and based on strong affective ties and they exist between children who are at similar developmental levels. Peer relationships, including friendships and relationships with parents, serve important functions in the child's life. Parents provide security and best friends satisfy needs of support, reassurance and comfort.

Factors influencing friendship formation

Friendships in real life are not conscious decisions but the result of some combination of similarity, proximity or circumstance. In adolescence, when one's friends help to define one's image, friendships may be the result of calculated decisions (Flashman, 2012). Some factors influencing friendships are as follows:

26 *Child-adolescent behaviour*

- *Similarity.* It is a very important factor and it means having similar ideas and values with the other person or being from the same social group, class, community or culture. According to Lindgren (1973), people are more attracted to those whose views, ideas and values resemble their own than to those whose views do not resemble their views. This is because holding similar views means that one does not have to explain or defend everything one says and getting agreement has a reinforcing effect. Further, there is more to talk about and less to argue and conversation is the social cement that keeps a friendship going. Izard (1960) found that personality test patterns of mutual friends were more similar than those of randomly selected pairs. The four subtypes of the kind of similarity leading to mutual attraction according to Miller (1963) are: "similarity of personality, similarity of traits that facilitate endeavours leading to a common goal, similarity in the ability of individuals to gratify the same needs in each other, and the possession of mutually-valued emotional commodities". Cairns et al. (1988) studied the social behaviour patterns of children of grades four to seven. Their results showed that children who were aggressive formed friendships with children who showed aggressive behaviour.
- *Propinquity.* It means frequently encountering the person informally, without making special plans to see each other. This leads to the development of friendships. This is because firstly, propinquity provides more opportunity to interact, and secondly, people feel a degree of similarity because they share the same residence area or have similar homes (Lindgren, 1973). Festinger et al. (1950) found that propinquity of residence was the major factor in determining who became friends with whom. Functional distance was more important than physical distance between apartments. For example, those who used the same stairs were more likely to become friends as they saw each other more often and were functionally closer. They had opportunities to share ideas and feelings with each other.
- According to Kennedy-Moore and McLaughlin (2017), three key ingredients of children's friendship formation are openness, similarity and shared fun. Friends tend to share common backgrounds, hobbies or interests and have similar demographics.

Sullivan's theory of friendship

The most often cited theory of friendship is Sullivan's "interpersonal theory" (Poulin and Chan, 2010). He explains how personality develops within interpersonal relationships. Every child goes through six developmental stages and interpersonal needs arise in each period of development. The six stages are:

Environment and the child's development 27

1. Infancy. Birth to 18 months.
2. Childhood. 18 months to 6 years.
3. Juvenile era. 6 to 9 years characterized by formation of peer groups.
4. Pre-adolescence. 9 to 12 years characterized by the development of relationships within the same gender.
5. Early adolescence. 12 to 14 years. This is the stage of identity formation.
6. Late adolescence. 14 to 21 years. It is the stage of formation of lasting intimate relationships.

Peer relations are central to adaptive development in the *juvenile period* with the need for companionship with peers. Interaction with peers gives children an opportunity to develop skills of competition, cooperation and compromise. The need for acceptance and the desire to avoid peer rejection that Sullivan labels "ostracism", emerge at this time. This becomes an important source of self-esteem or anxiety in the child. Children form in-groups and out-groups, they compare themselves to one another, they determine what behaviours and attitudes make valued companions and exclude those peers who do not meet these expectations.

Pre-adolescence is marked by the need for *interpersonal intimacy* that is satisfied through close friendship with a person of the same sex or chum. Mutuality is the key to this relationship. Friendship is based on closeness, self-disclosure, intimacy, shared experiences, reciprocity, similarity and collaboration that require sensitivity to the other person. In the juvenile era, peer relationships are not so intimate. A primary outcome of pre-adolescent friendship is validation of self-worth through self-disclosure. Children learn that their friends have similar interests, values and concerns, so they are important and worthy. Children recognize that they are valued by the other person. If they do not form a close friendship, loneliness results.

Role of friends in the child's development

- They give the child a sense of *emotional security*. Friends also help the child to learn how to control their emotions and respond to other's emotions. Ozturk's (2019) study findings indicated that the friendship qualities that students attached most importance to were trust, validation and support, self-disclosure, companionship and recreation. The least important dimensions of friendship qualities were help and guidance.
- Children learn from and teach *skills* to their friends. Friends provide socio-emotional resources such as companionship, support and validation so children show better adjustment in school as friends help in socio-emotional adjustment (Ladd et al., 1997).
- Children like to participate in some *activities* with friends who are similar to them. They may not enjoy doing those activities alone nor be happy if

28 *Child-adolescent behaviour*

parents do those activities with them. According to Lindgren (1973), the perception of similarities helps in the process of identity development as the traits that a child perceives in themself are reaffirmed when they are perceived in another. Interpersonal similarities facilitate social interaction and serve as the basis for communication, empathy, the development of group norms and cultural patterns of behaviour.

- Children turn to the *norms* laid down by their friends to discover the characteristics they should master. According to Sullivan, friendship plays an important role in the development of personal competence and identity and these features impact the adolescent's adjustment (Poulin and Chan, 2010).
- Children and adolescents learn *social skills* from their friends such as sharing, conflict resolution and communication skills. These are generalized to other relationships like work or relationship with a partner (Bagwell and Schmidt, 2011). They develop the ability to think through and negotiate different situations that arise in their relationships. According to Parker and Seal (1996), children without friends exhibit inadequate social skills.
- Friends set *standards* against which children can judge themselves. Children make their friends say how smart, kind, strong or attractive they are. Thus, they help the child to develop a self-concept. Flashman (2012) tried to understand the association between academic achievement and friendship ties made in high school students. Results showed that high-achieving students were more likely to extend ties to other high-achieving students. Low-achieving students made friendships with low-achieving students.
- According to Berndt, good friendships enhance a person's sense of *happiness* and overall well-being. Friends give support, they influence the child's behaviour, goals and attitudes through modelling or peer pressure and their influence affects the psychosocial development of the child positively or negatively (Poulin and Chan, 2010).
- Some *negative aspects of friendship* are conflict, rivalry, inequality, jealousy, social aggression between friends and deviancy training (Bagwell and Schmidt, 2011). Low friendship quality is associated with loneliness and depressive symptoms (Ladd et al., 1997).

Ferrer-Chancy and Fugate (2002) provide the following suggestions to parents to explain *how parents can help their child to make friends.*

A child is not born with social skills and may not know how to make friends. Since friends help children in their emotional, moral and social development and provide them with fun playmates, *parents should play an active role in helping their child to make friends.* They must prepare the child to interact successfully with peers. The most important thing they

Environment and the child's development   29

can do is to develop a loving, accepting and respectful relationship with their child. This warm relationship sets the stage for all future relationships including friendships. It helps the child to develop the basic trust and self-confidence necessary to go out and meet others. It develops a firm foundation on which the child can develop social skills. Parents can teach their children social skills by being good role models – that is, a child learns from how his/her parents interact with him/her and other people: how to meet people, to talk to them, to tell stories and jokes, to cooperate with others, to ask for favours, to apologize, to accept apologies, to win or lose well, to show appreciation or admiration, to accept compliments graciously, to be patient, respectful and considerate.

Some other ways in which *parents* can prepare their children are:

- Provide them with opportunities to spend time with other children and also encourage them to participate in games/sports.
- Teach the child to see the other person's point of view.
- Allow the child to resolve a fight with their friend on their own. They should step in only if absolutely necessary.
- Parents must remember that their child may have a different social style from their own. One style is not better than the other.

The impact of print media on the child

Parents must tell children stories/read out stories and encourage them to read stories and the newspaper because they have many *educational benefits*. They stimulate children's interest and curiosity, increase their thirst for knowledge and convey information about relationships. A study by Tsitsani et al. (2012) tried to find out about parents' opinions and children's preferences regarding storytelling. Children preferred to listen to fairy tales over modern stories. Most parents stated that children liked to listen to stories at least once a week.

Storytelling can be a special time for both parents and children as it helps to *build a good relationship* between parents and children. It allows parents to understand their children better.

Reading stories helps in the development of *language and thinking* in children. Young children can learn about size, colours, shapes, numbers and the world from picture books. Stories help the child to visualize spoken words and improve vocabulary and communication skills (Yabe et al., 2018).

Stories of birds and animals, adventures and mythological heroes boost the power of the *imagination and reasoning of the child* and encourage thinking. They teach the growing child lessons of morality and ethics and may instil faith and courage in them. According to the National Storytelling Network, USA, "Storytelling is the interactive art of using words and actions to reveal the elements and images of a story while encouraging the listener's imagination".

30   *Child-adolescent behaviour*

According to Yabe et al. (2018), there is frequent eye contact between the listener and the person telling the story in storytelling. Storytelling is different from picture book reading in the cognitive demands it makes on the listener in terms of imagination. Yabe et al. (2018) found that there was more sustained brain activation in storytelling in comparison with picture book reading. The picture book provides visual information to guide the listener's understanding so the listener does not have to imagine/visualize much.

Stories can help children to *deal with their feelings and stresses.* They touch the emotions of listeners and create smiles, excitement, sadness and/ or fears. For example, a child may hear a story about another child or animal being afraid of the dark and they understand that it is okay to be afraid of the dark. The child may also learn how to cope with this fear by reading a book. Books help the child to escape from stress for a while as the story takes their imagination to wonderful places.

When parents read out stories to their children they should also discuss how the characters might be feeling. According to Briers (2008), this helps to build their *emotional intelligence.* Briers says that parents can ask the child "Do you think he's feeling scared/cross/happy/upset?" This will expand the child's emotional vocabulary. According to Briers, parents must make children emotionally literate and teach them problem-solving skills and the importance of empathy. This will help children to have good mental health.

The kind of stories that interest children depends on their *age.* Two- and three-year-old children like their parents to tell them stories and they respond to their parents' voice, facial expressions, rhythmic sound, etc. Children between three and a half and five years like to handle story books themselves, see pictures, read alphabets and hear stories. A study by Tsitsani et al. (2012) found that children were positively affected by fairy tales and loved to hear about their favourite character again and again. Red Riding Hood was their favourite and they were happy when villains were punished.

The impact of television on the child

Children like to watch movies and television. Young children like to watch animated films, comedy and adventure. Older children also like to watch romantic and horror movies and television series.

Some *advantages* are:

- Movies take children to a whole new world by portraying interesting scenes and characters.
- Watching good television programmes offers new information, examples of good social behaviour, geographical and historical information and pleasant entertainment.

Environment and the child's development 31

Some *disadvantages* of watching too much television/movies are:

- It restricts the child's social interactions with their family and friends so the child makes little effort to develop their social skills. It makes children passive learners.
- It reduces physical activity in children since they spend long hours sitting in the same place. Hamer et al. (2009) found that higher levels of TV and screen entertainment time and low physical activity levels in young children interact to increase psychological distress in children.
- Excessive TV viewing in childhood has long-lasting adverse consequences for educational achievement in children and their subsequent socio-economic status and well-being (Hancox et al., 2005).
- If children watch aggression and violence regularly they may become more violent and aggressive in their behaviour. A study by Robertson et al. (2013) showed that watching television for too much time in childhood and adolescence resulted in increased anti-social behaviour and more aggressive personality traits in early adulthood. Bandura et al. (1961) found that children learn by observation and often imitate sequences of verbal and physical aggression that they see and they may even interact with inanimate objects like their toys or dolls in the same aggressive manner. Johnson et al. (2002) found a significant association between the amount of time spent watching television in adolescence and adulthood and the likelihood of subsequent aggressive acts against others.
- McAnally et al. (2019) found excessive TV viewing during childhood and adolescence (five to fifteen years) is a risk factor for developing an anxiety disorder in adulthood. It did not influence long-term risk for depression.
- Owens et al. (1999) studied the relation between television viewing practices and sleep disturbances in fourth-grade school children. The TV viewing habits associated most significantly with sleep disturbances were increased daily viewing TV time and increased TV viewing at bed time, especially in the context of having a TV set in the child's bedroom. The sleep domains affected by TV were sleep onset delay, anxiety around sleep and shortened sleep duration.

Since *overindulgence* in any *mass media* is not good, parents and teachers must monitor what their children read or watch. They must judge whether a book is within the understanding of the child and according to the child's ability and interest.

32 *Child-adolescent behaviour*

The influence of social media and the internet on the child

The use of social media has increased to a great extent in recent years in children, adolescents and adults. Social media in the form of social networking sites (SNS) is a current global phenomenon. Some social networking sites are Facebook, Instagram, WhatsApp and Snapchat. These are web-based services where individuals can create public or private profiles, connect with people across the world and share content.

The internet is one of the fastest ways for children and adolescents to get instantaneous news of events taking place across the globe and search for educational material on a wide range of topics, etc. If used properly and within limits, it makes people aware of happenings worldwide; it is educational, encourages community participation and improves connectivity. It helps people build social relationships, express their talents and improve their confidence. According to Prabhakararao (2016), "extroverts use SNS [social networking sites] for social enhancement, introverts use it for social compensation".

However, too much use causes problems. Adolescents who spend more than three hours per day on social networking sites may have mental health conditions like depression, anxiety or sleep disturbances (Prabhakararao, 2016). They may avoid going to school, not spend much time with family and friends, that is, not develop real-life social relationships. This may mean their social skills like the ability to listen and show empathy and kindness to people do not develop. Some harmful effects of too much social media are careless and aggressive behaviour, victimization to rumours, identity theft, stalking and cyber bullying.

According to Reid Chassiakos et al. (2016), some effects of TV, digital media and social media on children, based on evidence are:

- Early learning.
- Exposure to new ideas and knowledge.
- Increased opportunity for social contact and support.
- New opportunity to access health promotion messages and information.

Some disadvantages of media are:

- Negative effects on sleep, attention and learning.
- Higher incidence of physical health conditions like obesity.
- Mental health conditions like depression.
- Exposure to inaccurate, inappropriate or unsafe content and contacts.
- Compromised privacy and confidentiality.

So, parents should identify a balance of screen time, online time, studies and video games and set boundaries for children for accessing content. There should be consistent rules in the family about media use.

Environment and the child's development 33

Primac et al. (2009) found that more TV and total media exposure in adolescents were associated with increased odds of developing depressive symptoms in young adulthood. Casiano et al. (2012) found an association in adolescents between frequent screen time and obesity.

Daydreaming/mind-wandering and the child

Introduction

Daydreaming or mind-wandering (MW) occurs during a person's waking moments. According to Smallwood and Schooler (2015), MW means that the person is thinking of something that is unrelated to the activity being performed at that moment. According to Antrobus et al. (1966), MW is independent of perceptual stimuli. MW is self-generated thought or spontaneous thought that means cognitions arising through the shift of attention from ongoing events to more unconscious reflections and imagery (Baird et al., 2012). MW is a shift of attention away from external tasks towards internally generated thoughts (Unsworth and McMillan, 2013). MW is also called task-unrelated thought (TUT) (Cherry et al., 2022). A study by Killingsworth and Gilbert (2010) found that people spend 49.6 per cent of their time daydreaming, that is people are thinking about what is not happening almost as often as they are thinking about what is. They also found that doing so typically makes people unhappy. Giambra (2000) found that both the frequency and intensity of daydreaming decrease with age that is in adulthood. Stawarcszyk et al. (2014) found that adolescents experienced more frequent external distractions but no more MW than young adults. The cause of external distractions was poor concentration.

According to Singer (1975),

Daydreaming, our ability to give "to airy nothing a local habitation and a name", remains one of the least understood aspects of human behaviour. As children we explore beyond the boundaries of our experience by projecting ourselves into the mysterious worlds outside our reach. As adolescents and adults we transcend frustration by dreams of achievement or escape, and use daydreaming as a way out of intolerable situations and to help survive boredom, drudgery or routine. In old age we turn back to happier memories as a relief from loneliness or frailty, or wistfully daydream about what we would do if we had our time over again.

Singer states that the understanding of daydreaming and fantasy will give useful insights into the working of the human mind.

34 *Child-adolescent behaviour*

Benefits of daydreaming

The benefits of daydreaming if kept within bounds are:

- They are an aid to *adjustment* because they fulfil some of the child's wishes that cannot be fulfilled in reality. For example, children can fight imaginary battles and defeat people whom they may not be able to in real life. According to Klinger (1990), "Daydreams help us to get the most out of our brain power, and are an essential personal resource for coping with life". Thoughts on one's current problems or internal dialogues with real-life significant people may lead to positive solutions and coping strategies against stressful situations (Conte et al., 2023).
- Dreaming can be a secret world of the child that provides them with *excitement*.
- Daydreaming has positive values in *art, literature and invention*. It helps develop the child's creative thinking, finding meaning in personal experiences, planning future goals and activities (Stawarczyk et al., 2014). According to Baird et al. (2012), MW facilitates creative problem-solving. It can integrate the past and present experiences of a person and help with planning for the future.
- Imaginary friends may benefit a child's *language skills*. Singer (1998) found that daydreaming and acting out those daydreams in make-believe games serve an important information-processing function. Children, while trying to understand complex emotions and events for which they do not have life experiences, fill in the gaps by making up stories that reflect real situations.
- The kind of daydreams that a child has can provide an *insight* into their mental health and, accordingly, a trained psychiatrist or psychologist can help the child to deal with their problems. Conte et al. (2023) found that adolescents who showed excessive daydreaming also showed emotional symptoms, conduct problems and increased depressive, obsessive and post-traumatic stress problems.

Drawbacks of daydreaming

- It *consumes time*, so, if the child daydreams a lot, they cannot concentrate on their studies. When students do not pay attention because of TUT, they will miss acquiring crucial skills and knowledge (Smallwood and Schooler, 2015). MW interferes with performance on tasks that require sustained attention (Ottaviani and Couyoumdjian, 2013).

  According to Soemer et al. (2022), mind-wandering results in poorer reading comprehension in 13- and 14-year-old children (Soemer et al., 2022). They also found that children who were more interested in the

Environment and the child's development 35

topic showed reduced MW and better thinking and were more motivated readers.

- Cherry et al. (2022) found that daydreaming during a classroom-style listening activity had an unfavourable effect on the child's memory. Unsworth and McMillan (2013) found that differences in MW while reading were influenced by the child's working *memory* capacity, topic interest and motivation.
- If the child uses daydreams to cope with their difficulties frequently, it may not be good for the child if they are daydreaming to *avoid reality*. Frequency, intentionality and content are relevant factors in defining the functional meaning of daydreaming episodes. Sometimes children start imagining that they are ill, especially if they want attention or if they want to avoid an exam or going to school.
- Ottaviani and Couyoumdjian (2013) studied whether MW acted as a risk factor for health in an adult sample. They found that MW was linked to short-term health conditions such as increased heart rate on the same day and difficulty falling asleep on the subsequent night.

Types of daydream

According to Klinger (1990), two common themes that manifest often in children's daydreams are the "conquering hero" and "suffering martyr". In the *conquering hero* theme, the fantasy is of accomplishment, prestige or conquest. Children imagine themselves as a great person/hero, for example, as an athlete or a singer. They fantasize that they are the central character and all others pay homage to them. In the second theme, that is, the *suffering martyr*, children imagine themselves as a martyr, they see themselves as being unappreciated and misunderstood by others. They feel that other individuals are begging them for forgiveness. This type of daydream is an expression of self-pity. It is satisfying to the child for it is an adjustment to a lack of appreciation from others.

According to Soemer (2002), daydreaming is different from *maladaptive daydreaming*. Maladaptive daydreaming is intrusive and barely controllable and replaces real-life interactions. Having unpleasant experiences in childhood or social anxiety plays a role in maladaptive daydreaming. Social anxiety could lead to isolation and loneliness, leading to increased daydreaming. Sometimes maladaptive daydreaming can lead to poor social relationships and this could cause more anxiety in social situations.

According to Bigelsen et al. (2016), maladaptive daydreaming differs from daydreaming due to higher levels of unrealistic content, elevated recurrence, difficulties in controlling episodes and higher risk of affecting life goals; it is often accompanied by kinaesthetic activity.

4 Disciplining the child

Chapter outline

- Importance of discipline
- Discipline techniques
  - Types of discipline technique
  - Parents role in disciplining the child
- Parenting style
- Discipline and the teacher/school

Importance of discipline

Disciplining children is a very important responsibility of parents and teachers. The word "discipline" comes from the Latin word *"disciplina"* meaning instruction. According to the *APA Dictionary of Psychology* (VandenBos, 2015), "Discipline is training that is designed to establish desired habits of mind and behaviour. It means control of conduct, usually a child's, by means of punishment or reward". Disciplining the child means parents teach positive behaviour and try to change unwanted behaviour so that the child develops self-control and emotional maturity. Discipline means providing direction to the child with firmness. It is necessary to teach children about what is right and wrong, to train them to accept their social roles and responsibilities, to make them behave in accordance with social rules and become persistent and responsible adults. Discipline teaches children to use and channel their strengths and weaknesses to achieve something positive in life. The goal of discipline is to foster acceptable and appropriate behaviour in the child and ultimately lead to self-discipline (Nieman and Shea, 2004).

The child's school and teachers play an important role in disciplining children. For example, rules taught in the school like walking quietly from room to room or walking in a line to the assembly teach children to respect queues at a bus stop without pushing or acting in an unruly manner as they grow into adulthood. Similarly, the child has to be trained to sit quietly for periods of time in the classroom without chatting, joking or fidgeting.

DOI: 10.4324/9781003373070-4

Discipline techniques

Different techniques can be used by parents for disciplining namely verbal instructions and explanations, establishing rules, positive reinforcements like praise, approval and rewards, time-out and punishment. Discipline should be age appropriate (Banks and Quillen, 2002).

Types of discipline technique

- *Time-out.* This is a very effective method, especially for young children. Young children do not understand verbal instructions so time-out works well for them (Blum et al., 1995). Time-out should be used correctly for maximum effectiveness. It means sending a disruptive child to another room or to the corner of a room and they should not be given toys or video games, etc. The room should be neutral, safe and non-frightening. It should last for one minute per year of the child's age to a maximum of five minutes (Nieman and Shea, 2004). Time-out also means that the child and the undesirable/unwanted behaviour do not get parents' attention. Yet time-out is effective for a child only if they get their parent's attention otherwise. Such a child will miss being attended to. The child should be told which behaviour has caused the time-out.
- *Revoking privileges.* Depending on the child's age and personality, parents must limit access to the telephone, television, computer games, etc.
- *Ignoring undesired behaviour and giving positive reinforcement for desired behaviour.* Many times crying, sulking or quarrelling may cease if it fails to get parents' attention. Since the child does not get attention for that behaviour, the likelihood of its occurrence may gradually decrease (Skinner's theory of operant conditioning). Skinner's theory states that if an action is followed by a positive reinforcement/reward, it is likely to be repeated and learned. If an action is not followed by a positive reinforcement or reward the likelihood of its occurrence decreases (Morgan and King, 1975).
- *Verbal explanations*: Parents explain rules to the child clearly and provide direction. According to Hoffman (2000), "verbal explanations or inductive techniques when used with the child, promote internalization as they develop empathy and do not cause high level of fear or anxiety". The child understands the explanation and follows rules even when parents are not present. Too much or too little anxiety does not help in internalization. This is because very little anxiety may result in the child not attending to the parent's message. Too much anxiety interferes with the effective processing of the parental message about behavioural standards. Discipline techniques should arouse a moderate level of anxiety.

38 *Child-adolescent behaviour*

- *Rewards.* Rewards are a positive stimulus given to a person for a desirable response. According to the *APA Dictionary of Psychology* (VandenBos, 2015), "The word reward is used to describe the intent of someone providing a consequence for behaviour and it increases the frequency or probability of occurrence of the behaviour". Parents should use rewards carefully. A reward used to stop misbehaviour is a bribe. The child will try to get rewards from parents by misbehaving. Instead, parents should use rewards to appreciate some constructive behaviour displayed by the child. They can be rewarded verbally with words of praise or given a material reward like a chocolate, toys or extra privileges. Rewards should be given immediately after the act (Banks and Quillen, 2002). The token economy system (Ayllon and Azrin, 1965) can be used to provide positive reinforcement to a child. Children are given tokens for completing tasks or behaving in desired ways. After the child earns a certain number of tokens by engaging in desired behaviours, they can exchange these tokens to buy desired items.
- *Punishment*: According to the *APA Dictionary of Psychology* (VandenBos, 2015), "punishment is a physically or psychologically painful, undesirable or unwanted event or circumstance imposed as a penalty on an actual or perceived wrongdoer". Punishment can take different forms:
  - Verbal punishment. One example is scolding. It is used to express disapproval of the child's behaviour. If it is used frequently, the child may feel anxious and start avoiding their parents (Banks and Quillen, 2002). Parents should use verbal explanations to explain the mistake to the child in a firm and clear manner. Vissing et al. (1991) studied the effects of parents' verbal aggression on children of both genders from preschool to 18 years. Children who experienced verbal aggression from parents in the form of insults showed more physical aggression, delinquency and interpersonal problems than other children.
  - Withholding material things such as food-based treats and toys.
  - Corporal punishment (CP). "[CP] is defined as the use of physical force with the intention of causing a child to experience pain but not injury, for the purpose of correction or control of the child's behaviour. It can cause behavioural problems and slow down cognitive development" (Hornor et al., 2015). Corporal punishment should not be used because the child may imitate this behaviour and use it to cause pain to others; it can cause physical aggression, lower the child's self-esteem and confidence, cause emotional reactions such as depression, fear or anger and lead to poor academic performance.

Disciplining the child 39

- Taylor et al. (2010) found that children who were spanked by their mothers showed higher levels of aggression even after two years than those whose mothers did not use spanking.
- Straus et al. (1997) found that corporal punishment (spanking) by mothers increased anti-social behaviour in children aged six to nine years. Holmes and Robins (1988) found that children who went through harsh discipline and unfair punishment in childhood were more likely to experience feelings of depression or addiction to alcohol.
- According to Sege and Siegel (2018), positive parenting strategies of discipline should be used. Adults should avoid physical/corporal punishment and verbal punishment as they are minimally effective in the short-term and not effective in the long-term. Sege and Siegel state that some consequences of parental use of corporal punishment are:
  - Possibility of physical injury to the child.
  - Increased aggression in preschool and school-aged children.
  - The child may become defiant and aggressive in future.
  - The child may have cognitive problems or mental health conditions.
  - It may have a negative effect on the parent–child relationship.
- However, if appropriate punishment is used cautiously and sparingly, it can promote self-control without harming the child.
  - Punishment is most effective if it is administered immediately after the act for which the child is to be punished and if parents/teachers give the reason for the punishment to the child. It is effective if it is prompt, fair and consistent (Banks and Quillen, 2002).
  - The explanation must be at the child's level of understanding.
  - Excessive punishment should not be used because it gives children the feeling that they never do anything right, which is likely to lower their self-esteem. The child will feel unloved and resentful and may start avoiding the parent/teacher and it can also have harmful effects on the child's mental well-being.
  - Romana et al. (2015) found that children who were maltreated showed poorer academic performance and lower grades. They had emotional and behavioural difficulties like anxiety, aggression, low mood and poor interpersonal relationships.
  - Discipline should be given by an adult with an affective bond to the child (Nieman and Shea, 2004). This is because an important aspect that determines how the child reacts to punishment is the emotional relationship that the parent and child share. Punishment from a nurturing and affectionate parent is more likely to be effective than punishment from a cold,

40   *Child-adolescent behaviour*

withdrawn or hostile parent. This is because when an affectionate parent punishes a child, the child loses the parents' affection temporarily, which hurts them. The child stops the undesirable behaviour in order to regain the parents' affection. However, when the parent is hostile and cold, the punishment is not something different from the parents' usual behaviour. The child does not lose much emotionally when they are punished and so they make little effort to correct their behaviour.

Grusec and Goodnow (1994) state that "moral internalization means taking over the values and attitudes of the society as one's own so that socially acceptable behaviour is motivated not by anticipation of external consequences but by intrinsic/internal factors". They hold that power-assertive techniques or punishment are less effective than verbal explanations (reasoning) in promoting internalization because they elicit a high level of arousal in the child. Some power-assertive techniques are punishment, withholding privileges, withdrawal of love, which includes withholding attention, affection and approval.

According to Hoffman (2000), "power oriented techniques are detrimental to society as they arouse fear in the child, provide a model of aggression, direct the child's attention to the consequences of the behaviour for the self rather than other people".

According to Devi (2014), punishment does not teach the child the reasons for behaving correctly or the effects of their behaviour on others, it teaches the desirability of not getting caught.

According to the American Academy of Pediatrics (Sege and Siegel, 2018) adults caring for children should use healthy forms of discipline such as positive reinforcement for appropriate behaviours, setting limits, redirecting the child's behaviour and setting future expectations. Parents should not use physical and verbal punishment.

Parents must use positive discipline techniques as it respects the rights of the individual child and helps them to develop self-control. Positive discipline teaches the child what they should do. It differs from punishment because punishment indicates to a child what they should not do. Punishment can increase fear in the child whereas positive discipline may help the child to develop self-control. Some ways in which parents can use positive discipline with the child are:

1. To change an undesirable behaviour they should redirect the child to a new activity or change the focus of the child's behaviour.
2. They should point out the natural and/or logical consequences of the behaviour to the child.

Disciplining the child 41

3. They must teach the child acceptable ways to vent their feelings.
4. While providing verbal explanations to the child, they must focus on the inappropriate or undesirable behaviour and not on them as a person.
5. They must use time-out.
6. They must give the child focussed attention while helping them to deal with a particuar situation.

Positive discipline means:

1. Not using corporal punishment or verbal punishment
2. Not engaging in any form of neglect or child abuse
3. Not witholding opportunities for rest, food or sleep
4. Not telling the child to remain quiet for inappropriately long periods of time.

Parents role in disciplining their child

• They should not *praise* their child too much or too little. If parents praise the child too much, the child will expect lavish thanks for routine chores or be unable to finish even simple tasks without more approval. Dweck (2006) has done work on the "perils of praise" and found that children who were high in intelligence were quick to give up on challenging schoolwork. This is because all their life they had been told that they were smart. They did not want to contradict that evaluation by making a mistake. These children gave up as soon as they found something difficult. Dweck advises parents to praise children for effort, resilience and stamina rather than for being intrinsically intelligent. According to Briers (2008), "too much praise by parents will be devalued by children. So parents should not pay lip-service".

• Parents must not *over-criticize* the child because it may have an effect on the child's self-confidence. The child will find it difficult to respect and trust the parent (Nieman and Shea, 2004).

• They must *avoid heated words*. When children are fighting and misbehaving, parents feel angry and get upset. According to Briers (2008), parents should have a high level of self-control. This is because if they show emotional instability and anger, children will observe their parents' behaviour, and yelling is setting a bad example. Children learn many behaviours by imitation and identification (Bandura, 1977) and parents are their first role models. Saying "let me be calm, let me take charge of the situation" should be helpful or, to calm down, go for a walk. After some time, give the child a fair hearing and set limits for their behaviour.

42 Child-adolescent behaviour

- Parents *should not treat all children the same way*. The child's age and personality should colour the parents' discipline decisions as it has an impact on the child's social and emotional development (Banks and Quillen, 2002). A strong-willed child needs to be raised differently from a compliant child. If the child is daydreaming and gets distracted while cleaning their room, the parents must give the child specific instructions. For preschoolers, rules about respect for property and kindness to others should be taught. Children of school age respond to appeals to their sense of fairness. Discipline should be developmentally and temperamentally appropriate (Nieman and Shea, 2004).

- *Parents must not disagree* and argue with each other about discipline in front of the child because the child may feel insecure and will learn to play one parent off the other. According to Nieman and Shea (2004), parental disagreement can cause inconsistent discipline and make the child confused. Parents must be united when it comes to discipline (Banks and Quillen, 2002). Parents must agree with each other on general guidelines for children about homework, helping in household work, bedtime and also prohibitions against hitting, stealing and lying. Each parent must have authority in different realms so that one parent need not be responsible for all discipline.

- Parents must be *consistent in disciplining* the child. This means that it should not be that the parent punishes the undesirable act one day, ignores it on another day and praises it on yet another day. Neither should the undesirable behaviour displayed by the child be punished by one parent and let off by the other. This inconsistency in actions confuses the child and consequently the undesirable behaviour will persist.

- Parents must *allow children to voice their opinion* before making a decision. This has two benefits. Firstly, children will accept decisions better when they are at least consulted. Secondly, they will see themselves as a valued part of the whole family. Baldwin (1955) studied parent–child relationships and found that parents whose attitudes showed acceptance of the child and recognition of the child's rights and opinions were growth facilitating. They used rewards and clear rules for disciplining the child. Children showed emotional security, self-control and accelerated intellectual development. Children whose parents were strict and used punishment were rebellious, quarrelsome and showed aggressive behaviour.

- Parents must *focus on the child's actions* and not on them as a person. When parents discipline children they should make it clear that they are disapproving of that behaviour, not them. They must phrase corrections in specific terms such as, "You forgot to put away your shoes". This will let the child know that they can meet their parent's expectations in future even if they didn't meet them this time. If children use unacceptable words, parents must first find out as to where they picked up that word

Disciplining the child 43

and whether it is only an act of imitation by the child or the way in which the child is venting their unpleasant feelings.

- To *demonstrate their love and affection* to their children, parents must display some behaviours. They must:
  - Maintain eye contact while talking to them.
  - Maintain physical contact with the child, for example, patting them on the back.
  - Give the child focused attention, that is, spend time with each child separately.
  - Praise children on their accomplishments. Helper (1958) found that parental evaluations and acceptance influenced the child's self-evaluation. Children who felt that their parents' appraisal of them were positive, had positive feelings towards their bodies and their selves; those who felt appraisals were negative developed negative appraisals of their bodies and feelings of insecurity.
- Shinohara et al. (2012) found that that caregivers' praise of 18-month-old children played an important role in promoting a high-level trajectory of child social competence from eighteen months to three and a half years.

  Parents should supervise the child's friends to know whether they are moving around in bad company.
- Parents must *give the child time* to change their behaviour. According to Briers (2008), parents should understand that there is a connection between the child's thoughts, feelings and actions (behaviour). If a child is throwing things, parents must try to understand their thoughts and feelings at that moment about that situation and teach the child how to vent their feelings.

Parenting style

The way a child is disciplined can give an insight into the parenting style. Baumrind is considered a pioneer of research in parenting styles. According to Baumrind (1966), three parenting styles are authoritative parenting, authoritarian parenting and permissive parenting. Baumrind (1991) added a fourth parenting style: neglectful parenting. There is a difference in parent–child interactions and type of discipline techniques used in the four styles.

- *Authoritarian parents* are demanding. They expect their child to obey their orders and not ask for explanations. They provide rules that are clearly stated and do not encourage verbal give and take with the child. They favour punishment and forceful measures to make the child do what they think is right.
- *The permissive parent* is lenient, neither demanding nor directive and does not try to alter the child's behaviour. They do not exercise control and allow the child to regulate their own activities. They neither use

44   *Child-adolescent behaviour*

power nor coercion to get the child to obey rules and follow standards of behaviour.

- *Authoritative parents* set clear standards for the child and explain the reasons for these standards and rules. They are demanding but encourage the child to express themself or clarify doubts. This type of parent is firm, uses reason, power and reinforcement with the child. This type of discipline is supportive and not punitive.
- *Neglectful parents* make few demands on their children and are neither responsive nor nurturing. They do not enforce clear rules for children nor give them time and attention. They are indifferent to their children's activities and needs.

Authoritative parenting is the best style because the child is more likely to internalize the rules and follow them. Since parents are warm, caring, supportive and use praise, the child does not feel anxious. According to a study by Baumrind (1991), authoritative parents who were highly demanding and highly responsive were remarkably successful in protecting their adolescent children from problem drug use and in generating competence.

According to Steinberg et al. (1992), the authoritative parenting style, that is, high acceptance, supervision and psychological autonomy granting, is associated with positive developmental outcomes in adolescents like self-reliance, resilience, optimism, social competence, better school performance and academic achievement. They found that children of authoritarian parents show emotional reactions like anxiety, depersonalization, aggression and delinquent behaviours. Children of permissive parents show emotional reactions like anxiety, depression, withdrawn behaviour, school misconduct and delinquency. However, they also show characteristics like self-understanding and active problem-solving. Children of neglectful parents show least-favourable outcomes such as inadequate social and school competence, low self-esteem, anxiety and delinquency. They did not display self-regulation and social responsibility.

According to Maccoby and Martin (1983), two key dimensions of parenting are responsiveness and demandingness. Responsiveness is the extent of parental warmth, acceptance and involvement. Demandingness is the extent to which parents are strict and controlling. Based on a combination of these two dimensions of demandingness and responsiveness, they defined four parenting styles. They are:

- *Authoritative style*: High demandingness and high responsiveness.
- *Authoritarian style*: High demandingness and low responsiveness.
- *Permissive style*: Low demandingness and high responsiveness.
- *Neglectful style*: Low demandingness and low responsiveness.

Disciplining the child 45

Discipline and the teacher/school

According to Wankat and Oreovicz (2015), some common discipline problems that teachers have to handle are students talking in the class instead of paying attention to the teacher, wearing headphones, coming late, absenteeism, missing tests or exams, procrastination, arguing and asking for more marks, trying to buy marks by doing favours or giving gifts to the teacher, cheating in exams, lying or stealing. For all these problems, taking some preventive measures is the best course of action.

Cheating is common during exams or assignments. Starovoytova and Arimi (2017) conducted a survey to study cheating in exams in a school of engineering students. They found that only 18 per cent of the students admitted that they had never cheated but had witnessed their classmates cheating. The students who cheated did so to avoid failing and to get good marks. They were not bothered about being caught while cheating. Starovoytova and Arimi concluded that the reason for this is the penalties for cheating were not enough of a deterrent to cheating.

Wankat and Oreovicz (2015) hold that the teacher should create a conducive atmosphere to prevent students from cheating. The teacher should create good rapport with students, teach well, encourage students to ask questions and clear their doubts, should be impartial and not over-strict in corrections. They should teach students techniques to reduce exam-related anxiety so students will not feel like they need to cheat.

Some measures can be taken by teachers to prevent misbehaviour:

- The teacher must explain to the students the rules that they have to follow and the penalty for coming late to class, excessive absenteeism, missing exams/make-up exams and cheating in exams.
- Teachers must be polite but firm with students and treat them with respect.
- The teacher must not openly compare students with each other.
- The teacher must try to know students' names, use their names in class and also make classes interactive as it holds students' attention.
- The teacher must praise and reward students for good performance and behaviour. They should not humiliate students with poor performance but help them to understand their mistakes.

In school, children are disciplined using some positive reinforcement techniques like praise or verbal approval, a smile, rewards like material items, medals, certificates or extra privileges. Some power-oriented techniques that are used are withholding approval or recognition, verbal punishment, sending them out of class, not allowing students to attend school (suspension) or participate in games for a fixed time period. The teacher should give verbal

46 Child-adolescent behaviour

explanations to students with all the reinforcement techniques, so the child will know what they did wrong . Sometimes informing the child of the possibility of failing in a test unless one studies can be used to discipline students. This technique should be used sparingly and cautiously. The teacher should not scold or criticize students in front of other students for their mistake as this will demoralize them and they may develop resentment, rebelliousness and a negative attitude towards teachers and the school. The child's desire to learn and any interest in particular subjects may decrease. A sound value-based ethical education should be made part of the curriculum to teach children the difference between right and wrong.

5 Development of children's ambitions and aspirations

Chapter outline

- Introduction
- Level of aspiration
  - Factors influencing children's level of aspiration
    - Personal factors
      - Psychological needs
      - Need for achievement
      - Child-rearing practice
      - Parental warmth
      - Modelling
      - Conscientiousness
      - Socio-economic status
      - Self-esteem
      - Self-efficacy
    - Environmental factors
      - Parental behaviour
      - Teacher influence

Introduction

One of the most important, difficult and crucial decisions that a person has to make is to 'single out' a career or a course of study for themselves, keeping in mind their interests, abilities and circumstances and choices available. There are differences between children/adolescents in their choice of their career and this depends on their ambitions, aspiration level and goals. Hoppe (1930) defines level of aspiration (LOA) as "a person's expectations, goals or claims on his own future achievement in a given task". There are many causes for these differences in a person's selection of their career/course of study. For instance, children may wish to take up the profession of a doctor because:

- Their parents are doctors and they see it as a good way to make a living.
- Their childhood curiosity about bodily functions was never satisfied.

DOI: 10.4324/9781003373070-5

48 *Child-adolescent behaviour*

- In their play activities as children they obtained satisfaction out of doctoring other children with the aid of a doctor's kit.
- They want to serve mankind.
- Their friends are going to be doctors.
- Sometimes it could be a combination of these influences.
- The motive could be a desire in children for mastery, self-assertion or recognition, or it could be a desire to be independent or the need for achievement.

Some other factors that may cause differences in the person's selection of their career are: parental pressure, family circumstances, financial problems, physical and mental health of the child, physical and mental disabilities and aptitudes of the child. Sometimes the child/adolescent does not know what their interests are or the alternatives that are available. They may experience "role confusion" in Erikson's (1980) words. Details of Erikson's psychosocial theory of development can be found in Chapter 9 of this book.

Level of aspiration

When a person comes across a huge boulder in their path obstructing the way, they can do one of three things: they can push it aside, go around it or go back to see if they can take a new route altogether. Similarly, in choosing life's goals or one's career or in undertaking everyday activities, children differ in their level of aspiration, that is, in their expectations of accomplishment or in the demands they make upon themselves. The concept of LOA was first used by Dembo and defined by Frank (1941) as "The level of future performance on a familiar task which an individual, knowing his level of past performance in that task explicitly undertakes to attain".

Gardner (1940) defined LOA as "truly a quantitative concept, which has two requirements; that the subject makes some public indication of his aims and that he makes this in quantitative terms".

LOAs are influenced by children's attitudes towards themselves and by their estimate of group status. The level of aspiration appears clearly after children have formed some conception of themselves, that is, after they have developed a sense of pride that they feel must be maintained.

According to Hoppe (1930), success and failure in attaining their goals make children modify their level of aspiration. He describes two types of shifts in level of aspiration:

1. *Typical shifts* mean that the level of aspiration is raised when performance attains the level of aspiration and lowered when performance falls below the level of aspiration.

Children's ambitions and aspirations 49

2. *Atypical shifts* in level of aspiration mean an increase in level of aspiration after failure and a decrease in level of aspiration after success. An individual's aspiration level influences their personality and adjustment.

According to Coleman (1981),

the pursuit of unrealistically high goals leads to failure and frustration; the pursuit of goals that are too low leads to wasted opportunities and lost satisfactions; the pursuit of false goals leads to disillusion and discouragement. Well-adjusted people tend to have a reasonably accurate view of themselves in relation to their world and hence to have a fairly realistic level of aspiration. Maladjusted people, on the other hand, tend to be unrealistic – to set their goals too high or too low or to pursue unrewarding goals. In many cases, maladjusted people seem unable to formulate meaningful life plans and goals and drift through life with little or no sense of direction and experience feelings of dissatisfaction, aimlessness, and being lost.

Mohanty (1978) studied differences between male and female college students in shifts and rigidity in level of aspiration. Their results revealed that females showed more typical responses than males. They also indicated flexibility in their level of aspiration behaviour by increasing the level of aspiration with success and lowering the level of aspiration with failure in comparison to their male counterparts.

Factors influencing children's level of aspiration

Personal factors and environmental factors influence the level of aspiration.

1. Some *personal factors* that influence children's level of aspiration are their wishes, interests, values, needs, motives, goals, personality type, conscientiousness, self-esteem, self-efficacy, past experience and socioeconomic status.
2. Some *environmental factors* that influence children's level of aspiration are parental behaviour, ambitions and education level, social expectations, cultural traditions, mass media, social values, social rewards and punishment and competition with peers and siblings, school and teachers.

Personal factors

Psychological needs

A person's aspirations and ambitions are influenced by some psychological needs. *APA Dictionary of Psychology* (VandenBos, 2015), "a psychological need is any need that is essential to mental health or that is not a biological necessity". These needs are closely related to the goals that a person sets for themself and also play an important role in motivating their behaviour.

50 *Child-adolescent behaviour*

According to *McClelland's "needs theory" (1987)*, three important needs that influence a person's aspirations and goal-setting behaviour, that is, three motivating drives are the needs for achievement, affiliation and power. These needs are not inborn but develop over time as children grow up. One motive dominates and this dominant motivator is influenced by a person's experiences with different people, their environment and cultural opinion. The strength of these needs differ from person to person and influence three things: how a person approaches and tackles problems, interpersonal relationships and the kind of risks they take.

1. The need for *affiliation* refers to the desire in a person to interact and socialize with others, especially peers, to please others, to seek harmonious relationships with others and to win affection and appreciation from others. Those high in the need for affiliation seek to work in groups and create friendly and lasting relationships. Maintaining good relationships is important and they favour collaboration over competition. They do not like situations with high risk and they adhere to norms and rules.
2. The need for *power* refers to a person's need to excel in one's work, to compare one's skills with competitors, to achieve respect and recognition from people and to dominate and control people. Those high in the need for power are high in the need for achievement. They enjoy competition, winning arguments and influencing others. They have a constant need for better personal status and they are interested in prestige, recognition and controlling others.
3. The need for *achievement* means striving for success or the desire to perform well. According to McClelland (1987), "Achievement motivation is affect in connection with evaluated performance in which competing with a standard of excellence is paramount".
    The *achievement motivation theory* by *McClelland (1953)* and *Atkinson (1957)* is a theoretical model that explains how the motive to achieve and the motive to avoid failure influence a person's behaviour in a situation where performance is evaluated against some standard of excellence (Atkinson and Feather, 1966). According to McClelland and Atkinson, achievement oriented activity is activity undertaken by an individual with the expectation that the performance will be evaluated in terms of some standard of excellence. Achievement oriented activity is always influenced by the resultant of a conflict between two opposed tendencies, the tendency to achieve success and the tendency to avoid failure.

They also distinguish between two types of individuals: one type is high in the need for achievement but low in the motive to avoid failure, the other type is

Children's ambitions and aspirations 51

low in the need for achievement but high in the motive to avoid failure as they are dominated by their anxiety.

Persons who are high on the need for achievement like to set challenging goals and test their competencies. They are attracted to tasks that are moderately difficult and they take calculated risks. They are attracted to success and not afraid of failure. They are not interested in attempting tasks that are very easy, as they offer little challenge. They are also not interested in attempting tasks that are very difficult and risky as the possibility of failure is more. They want to excel as this gives them personal satisfaction. While working, they prefer to be independent. They like to receive feedback on their progress.

Persons scoring low on need for achievement have low self-confidence and low opinion about their abilities. They attempt low risk tasks as chances of failures are less. They also are attracted to high risk tasks as winning in such tasks is anyway a matter of luck.

- **Need for achievement:** The strength of the achievement motive in children affects their level of Aspiration. The need for achievement varies from person to person. Those high on the need for achievement are found in positions involving high risk taking and responsibility.

Lindgren (1973) defines achievement need as follows

The need for Achievement refers to accomplishment: mastering, manipulating, and organizing the physical and social environment; overcoming obstacles and maintaining high standards of work; competing through striving to excel one's previous performance, as well as rivalling and surpassing others and the like.

Richardson and Abraham (2009) conducted a study to investigate predictors of university students grade point average (GPA) using male and female students over nine months. They measured the achievement motivation, and the big five personality traits: extraversion, agreeableness, openness, conscientiousness and neuroticism. Their results revealed that conscientiousness and achievement motivation explained the variation in GPA for both male and female students.

Sepulveda et al. (2021) found that adolescents who had a sense of purpose had higher self-efficacy and consequently were more committed to academics. They took help from others, tried to increase their competencies and knowledge. This motivated them to engage in behaviours that led to academic achievement.

52 Child-adolescent behaviour

Nelson and DeBacker (2008) found that adolescents who perceived that they were respected by their classmates and those who had a best friend who valued academics, showed adaptive achievement motivation. Factors responsible for variation in the need for achievement are:

- **Child-rearing practice**: According to psychologists Donelson and Gullahorn (1977), for both boys and girls, achievement orientation is enhanced by authoritative parental behaviour. The authoritative pattern involves sensitivity to the child's maturity and abilities, clear communication of expectation and use of reason with some punishment, but not with restrictive or coercive behaviour towards the child. Forcing children to do something or giving punishment may not induce the achievement motive in school children. Criticisms like, "You cannot do this", should not be used by parents as it will hurt children and discourage them from trying. To induce the mastery motive in their children, parents must give ample support and reassurance of their abilities and help them to sequence the strategies for success.

Aunola et al. (2000) conducted a study to understand if there is an association between parenting style and adolescents' academic achievement and performance. The results showed that adolescents from authoritative families applied adaptive achievement strategies characterized by low levels of failure expectations, task irrelevant behaviour and passivity and they used self-enhancing attributions. Adolescents from neglectful families applied maladaptive strategies characterized by high levels of task irrelevant behaviour, passivity, and they did not use self-enhancing attributions.

- **Parental warmth**: A moderate level of warmth and nurturance by parents' fosters achievement behaviour. Too much affection and protection by parents or too many restrictions diminish children's achievement behaviour. An important factor that determines the academic aspirations of children is the expectation of parents for the educational achievements of their child. This means that parents place high value on independence, mastery and competence.

Rogers et al. (2009) examined the association between children's perceptions of their parents' educational involvement, children's personal characteristics and their school achievement. The father's academic pressure on the child predicted lower achievement but mother's encouragement and support predicted higher achievement. Both parents used more academic pressure with their sons, but more encouragement and support with their daughters. This study showed the interaction of parents' educational involvement and children's personal characteristics in predicting school achievement.

Children's ambitions and aspirations 53

- **Modelling**: According to Bandura (1977), observation and modelling play an important role in why and how children learn and also in their aspirations and level of achievement. Parents are the first role models for the child. The extent to which the child identifies positively with parental models plays a role.

According to Hurlock (1976),

> In identification the child wants to think, feel and act in a manner which he believes is representative of the standards of the cultural group as shown in the person he selects as his model. Identification is self-initiated and inner controlled.

According to Stoke, "Identification occurs when a person gives his 'emotional allegiance' to the model, that is, the person he admires and wants to resemble, whether that person be a parent, a teacher, a peer or a popular hero" (cited in Hurlock, 1976). So the quality and strength of the parent-child relationship is important. More the admiration and affection a child has for a parent, the more he identifies with the parent. Sometimes the child may find identification with either parent difficult or impossible and in such cases will try to be as unlike them as possible.

Some other role models are the child's siblings, friends, classmates, senior students in the school, teachers, neighbours, relatives, leaders and public figures. Flashman (2012), study among high school students showed that high achieving students were more likely to extend ties to other high achieving students. Low achieving students made friendships with low achieving students.

Chesters and Daly (2017) conducted a study on secondary school students to examine associations between parental education, school attended and level of educational attainment. They found that children whose parents were university educated had higher achievement level than students whose parents were not highly educated. Another finding was that attending a school with higher number of educationally disadvantaged families had a negative effect on the educational achievement of the child.

- **Conscientiousness**: It is one of the Big Five personality traits of the Five Factor model. According to McCrae and Costa it means being reliable, ambitious, organized, hard-working, self-disciplined and persevering (Verbree et al. 2023).

Verbree et al. (2023) examined the factors causing greater success in higher education in post-graduate students. They explain the gap in achievement level between the genders as being due to differences in 'conscientiousness' which was higher in females.

54 *Child-adolescent behaviour*

Kertechian (2018) studied the relation between academic motivation, conscientiousness, procrastination, and academic performance in university students of management. Their results showed that students with higher grade point average were high in conscientiousness, were intrinsically motivated and procrastinated less. They concluded that among the management students, the personality trait of 'conscientiousness' is the best predictor of academic achievement.

- **Socio-economic status (SES)**: According to the APA Dictionary of Psychology (VandenBos, 2015), socio-economic status is defined as the position of an individual or group on the socio-economic scale, which is determined by a combination of social and economic factors such as income, amount and kind of education, type and prestige of occupation, place of residence and in some societies or parts of society – ethnic origin or religious background.

The child's socio-economic status determines the strength of the need for achievement. Parents of different economic groups vary in their academic expectations from their children. Parents of middle and upper income groups are more likely to encourage their children to work hard in school and succeed academically.

Brown and Putwain (2022) studied how gender and socio-economic status relate to achievement. The sample consisted of students who were in the final year of upper secondary education. Their results showed that parental education was directly related to achievement. Gender and socio-economic status were indirectly related to achievement. Males and students whose parents had higher education level and students who had more possessions in their household performed better in their examination. They explained these differences as being due to higher expectations of the students for success and subjective task value.

Selvitopu and Kaya (2021) conducted a meta-analysis to find out the relation between socio-economic status and academic performance of school children (pre-primary and secondary). In an effort to measure socio-economic status they assessed income of the family, parental occupation, and home resources. They found a moderate positive correlation between socio-economic status and academic performance.

- **Self-esteem:** According to Coopersmith (1967), "self-esteem is the evaluation an individual makes and customarily maintains with regard to the self." It is the need in children to feel good about themselves and worthy of respect of others. His study found that children who had high self-esteem were more assertive, independent, creative, flexible, and capable of more original solutions to problems than children with low self-esteem. A child's self-esteem influences his self-confidence,

Children's ambitions and aspirations 55

academic performance, adjustment and desire to compete. According to Coleman (1981),self-esteem has its early foundation in parental affirmation of worth and in mastery of early developmental tasks; it receives continual nourishment from the development of new competencies and achievement in areas deemed important; and eventually it comes to depend heavily on the values and standards of significant others. If a person measures up to those standards in terms of physical appearance, achievement, or economic status – he can approve of himself and feel worthwhile.

Acosta-Gonzaga (2023) studied the effects of academic motivation and self-esteem on academic performance of University students. Their results indicated that motivation of students affects their academic performance, as it makes students plan their study and use learning strategies. The self-esteem level of students affects students' feelings and behaviours. Those with low self-esteem show emotions like sadness and anxiety and behaviours like mental detachment and poor concentration.

Joshi and Srivastava (2009) studied self-esteem and academic achievement of urban and rural adolescents and gender differences in self-esteem and academic achievement. They found no significant difference in self-esteem level of rural and urban adolescents. They found significant differences between rural and urban adolescents in academic achievement with urban adolescents having higher scores. Girls scored significantly higher than boys on academic achievement. Boys scored significantly higher on self-esteem than girls.

- *Self-efficacy (SEFF)*: According to Bandura (1977), self-efficacy refers to people's judgement of their capabilities to organize and execute courses of action required to attain designated types of performances. It is one's belief in one's ability to succeed in specific situations. It plays a major role in how one approaches goals, tasks and challenges.

He holds that self-efficacy influences academic achievement.

According to Bandura (1977), there are four factors that affect a person's self-efficacy and they influence the person's aspirations and achievement. The four factors are as follows:

1. Past performance and mastery experiences influence confidence and self-efficacy. Success enhances self-efficacy and failure lowers it.
2. Modelling or vicarious experience: When we see people/social models like parents, teachers, peers or people similar to oneself accomplishing a task, we start believing that we can also perform the same task. If that person succeeds and we observe this, our self-efficacy increases. If the other person fails, our self-efficacy decreases.

56 *Child-adolescent behaviour*

3. Verbal persuasion: It refers to providing direct encouragement to a person, that is, telling him/her ("you can do it") or discouragement ("you cannot do it"). When a significant person provides encouragement to us it increases our self-efficacy; if a significant person discourages us it decreases our self-efficacy.

4. Physiological factors: A person's physical abilities, aches and pains, moods and stress levels affect their judgement of personal efficacy. A person who has low self -efficacy will interpret aches and pains as a sign of inability to perform and this will decrease his self-efficacy further; a person with high self-efficacy will interpret aches and pains as unrelated to ability.

Bhatt and Bahadur (2018) studied college students and found that there was a strong positive correlation between students' self-efficacy, self-esteem and their achievement motivation. They state that motivation is important for students as it directs their behaviour towards goals, affects their choice of goals, leads to increased effort, makes them persist in the activity and improves their concentration and interest in what they are learning.

Environmental factors

Parental behaviour

To enhance the child's achievement orientation and to make them an academic achiever, parents should:

*   Place high value on autonomy, mastery, competence and achievement of their children.
*   Reinforce achievement efforts of children with affection and praise regardless of the outcomes. This will strengthen their belief in themselves.
*   Be democratic with children, that is, encourage an active give-and-take interaction with them, communicate their expectations and tell them the importance of setting realistic goals.
*   Exhibit a moderate level of warmth and nurture to their children, curiosity towards their activities and a respect for their knowledge and abilities.
*   Parents should avoid comparing their child with their classmates or siblings.
*   They must be a model of high achievement for their children by displaying achievement behaviours themselves.

Teacher influence

Some *motivational techniques* that teachers can use to motivate students so that they do their best and raise their level of aspiration are rewards, marks

Children's ambitions and aspirations 57

and grades, praise, competition and cooperation and punishment. Punishment should be used carefully and sparingly by the teacher. Rewards may be either symbolic like gold stars, medals and certificates or material like cash, books, sweets, etc. Rewards give status and impel students to greater activity. Rewards should be given immediately after the act (Banks and Quillen, 2002). More details of "the effects of rewards and punishment on children" are provided in Chapter 4 of this book.

Marks and grades (feedback) are useful because they inform students of their progress and they can compare it with their own performance (Margolis and McCabe, 2006). This information about their progress leads to a sense of self- competition and is a strong incentive to further effort. Praise is an incentive to effort for students of all ages. It could be verbal or just a handshake or pat on the back. The teacher should induce competition between students by keeping in mind that there should be a degree of equality among the competitors. Each student must have some chance of winning. The teacher can also arrange group/squad competitions between students. This will make them learn to cooperate and to work as a team to make their group win. Cooperative learning strategies promote self-evaluation and hence improve both self-efficacy and academic achievement (Bandura, 1977).

According to Margolis and McCabe (2006), some *tips* for a teacher to improve self-efficacy and motivation in students are:

- Use moderately difficult tasks, slightly above students' current ability level.
- Use peer models since students can learn by watching a peer succeed at a task.
- Teach students specific learning strategies like working on an assignment or a project.
- Capitalize on students' interests by linking the course material or concepts to their interests in culture, technology, etc.
- Allow students to make some choices, for example, give assignment options.
- Give students consistent, credible and specific encouragement.
- Give students frequent focused feedback regarding their performance and compare it with their own past performance.
- Teachers must themselves have a high sense of self-efficacy about their teaching capabilities.

6 Developing the child's creativity

Chapter outline

- Definition
- Characteristics of creative children/adolescents
- Differences between creative thinking and intellectual thinking
- Development of creative talent
- Factors influencing creativity
- Parents' role in encouraging creative thought
- Tips for teachers
- The education system and creativity
- Barriers to creativity

Definition

According to the *APA Dictionary of Psychology* (VandenBos, 2015),

> Creativity is the ability to produce or develop original work, theories, techniques or thought. Creative thinking is the mental process leading to a new invention, solution or synthesis in any area. Products of creative thinking include new machines, social ideas, scientific theories and artistic works.

Creativity is the process of thinking originally, recombining ideas in new ways and breaking away from set ways of thinking and behaviour. Creative thought appears in all aspects of life – from the way a parent quiets a crying child to the methods a scientist uses to discover a cure for a disease. Creative thinking is characterized by originality, that is, the rarity or uniqueness of the response; by fluency, that is, the number of responses that the person makes; by flexibility, that is, the number of types of responses that the person makes. "To create" means to bring something new into existence.

The father of creativity, Ellis Paul Torrance, defined creativity as "the capacity to detect gaps, propose various solutions to solve problems, produce novel ideas, re-combine them, and intuit a novel relationship between ideas" (Almeida et al., 2008). He developed the Torrance Tests of Creative Thinking

DOI: 10.4324/9781003373070-6

Developing the child's creativity 59

(TTCT) to assess an individual's creative potential. It has two forms, figural and verbal. The figural TTCT assesses five mental characteristics – fluency, originality, elaboration, abstractness of titles and resistance to premature closure. The verbal TTCT includes three parts that assess fluency, i.e., the number of relevant responses; flexibility, i.e., the number of different categories of relevant responses; originality, i.e., statistical rarity of responses.

Kaufman and Beghetto (2009) propose a Four C model of creativity consisting of the following:

- Little-c or creativity recognized by people in the immediate environment (leading to productions that are out of the ordinary).
- Big-c, that is, legendary creativity (enduring creativity recognized on a very large scale).
- Mini-c, self-recognized creativity (exploration activities through new experiences).
- Pro-c, creativity recognized by experts in the field.

According to Drevdahl (1956),

Creativity is the capacity of persons to produce competitions, products or ideas of any sort which are essentially new or novel and previously unknown to the producer. It can be an imaginative activity or thought synthesis where the product is not a mere summation. It may involve the forming of new patterns and combinations of information derived from past experience and the transplanting of old relationships to new situations and may involve the generation of new correlates. It must be purposeful or goal-directed, not idle fantasy, though it need not have immediate practical application nor be a perfect and complete product. It may take the form of an artistic, literary or scientific production or may be of a procedural or methodological nature.

Characteristics of creative children/adolescents

- They are especially observant and value accuracy in observation.
- They perceive things as others do but they also perceive things as others do not.
- Their thinking is more independent than that of others and they spend a lot of time thinking.
- Their thinking is capable of involving many ideas at one time and of synthesizing them in a unique and unusual way.
- Their thinking reveals a great use of imagination and fantasy.
- They are experimentative by nature.

60 *Child-adolescent behaviour*

- They never rest on their oars nor are they satisfied with one way of doing things.
- They always pursue and persist searching for better and faster means, methods and uses.
- They are fired by the urge to stray away from the beaten path; they are flexible and avoid monotony.
- Creative persons are inquisitive, persistent, independent and they like to take risks.

According to Almeida et al. (2008), some personality characteristics of a creative person are an open mind, novelty, tolerance to ambiguity and cognitive functions like ideational fluency and thinking flexibility. According to Corazza (2016), creativity is a dynamic phenomenon. Cognitive and affective energy is required in the decision to engage in creative activity and dynamic relationships with the environment bear fundamental influences on the process. As the creative process is dynamic, it produces typically multiple outcomes over time. For a given creative production, creative inconclusiveness and creative achievement can alternate in time and at the same time. Creative achievement and inconclusiveness can coexist across different cultural domains.

Differences between creative and intellectual thinking

- In intellectual thinking, correctness matters; in creative thinking, the wealth of ideas is important.
- Intellectual thinking is selective; creative thinking is generative.
- Intellectual thinking is analytical; creative thinking is provocative.
- Intellectual thinking moves in an established direction; creative thinking creates direction.
- Intellectual thinking follows the most likely path; creative thinking explores the least likely path.
- Intellectual thinking is closely related to reality; creative thinking involves the use of imagination and fantasy.

Xiaoxia (1999) studied the possible relation between creativity and academic achievement in school students and also studied whether there are gender differences in this relation. The students were administered a creative test battery and teachers rated the students' creativity. The teachers' ratings showed that creativity was related to academic achievement for both boys and girls. For boys, flexibility was the predominant factor that related to all academic subject areas. For girls, elaboration and fluency related to academic subject areas. However, creativity was barely related to academic achievement as per the students' performance on the tests.

Developing the child's creativity 61

Furnam (2008) conducted a study on adults to investigate the relationship between intelligence quotient, emotional quotient and creativity. Cognitive ability was positively but not significantly correlated with divergent thinking (creativity) and it was significantly negatively correlated with emotional intelligence scores.

Development of creative talent

The way in which creativity in children develops depends both on their heredity and environment. Children who are unwilling to experiment, who are resistant to suggestions and do not want to think afresh are not likely to be creative. Besides, the creative ability in a child can be increased in a supportive climate, that is, encouragement from the child's parents, teachers and education system. Sometimes the creative talent of a child does not develop because the child has physical health problems or has to face environmental hurdles. According to Lucas (2001), there are four keys to fostering creative learning:

- The need to be challenged by setting goals and supported in reaching those goals.
- The elimination of negative stress.
- The ability to live with uncertainty.
- The importance of receiving feedback (Massie et al., 2022).

According to the "investment theory of creativity and its development" by Sternberg and Lubart (1991), the six resources for creativity are intellectual processes, knowledge, intellectual style, personality, motivation and environmental context. Creative performance results from a confluence of these elements. Creativity is a decision to "buy low and sell high" in the realm of ideas, meaning creative individuals identify and pursue novel, initially unpopular ideas, ultimately reaping the benefits of their unconventional thinking.

According to Arasteh (1968), there are *"critical periods"* in the development of creativity in a child. They are critical in the sense that, if the development of the child's creativity is obstructed in this stage it may be suppressed and not manifest.

- The first critical period is between five and six years. Children learn that they have to accept authority and discipline. Since they have to conform, their creativity may not develop.
- The second critical period is between eight and ten years. The desire to be accepted as a member of their peers, reaches its peak at this stage. To be accepted by their peers, children feel they have to conform and so they might give up their creative interests.

62   *Child-adolescent behaviour*

- The third critical period is between 13 and 15 years. As in the previous stage, children strive for approval from their peers and also members of the opposite sex. They conform with the hope that they will be accepted and may give up their creative interests.
- The fourth critical stage is between 17 and 19 years. In this stage adolescents want to be accepted by their peer group. So to "fit in" they may conform to the norms and ideas of the peer group and give up their creative interests.

Factors influencing creativity

Some factors that cause individual differences in creativity are family atmosphere, ordinal position and personality of the child, teacher and method of education, socio-economic status and type of environment (rural/urban).

Studies were conducted to understand *how the family influences the development of creativity* in a child. A study by Jankowska and Gralewski (2002) found that a constructive parenting style was positively related to the development of the child's creativity in children between 6 and 12 years of age. The constructive parenting style consisted of parental acceptance of the child, autonomy granting, encouragement to experience novelty and variety, support of perseverance in creative efforts and encouragement to fantasize in the parent-child relationship. According to Sing et al. (2023), parents who balance guidance with allowing children freedom for exploration positively influence their child's creativity.

Yang et al. (2017) investigated the differences in cognition (intelligence and creativity), personality and anatomical structural differences of grey matter volume (GMV) between only children and non-only children. Only children scored higher on flexibility (a dimension of creativity) and lower on agreeableness (a personality trait) than non-only children. There were significant differences in GMV between only children and non-only children that occurred in some brain regions that are related to these dimensions of creativity and agreeableness. They suggest that family environment may play an important role in the development of the behaviour and brain structure of children.

Yeh et al. (2023) compared rural and urban elementary school children's creativity performance. They also studied the learning effect of digital game-based creative learning. They found that urban, middle-class students outperformed the rural students in the creativity test before game-based learning. But after game-based learning, all children got a higher score on the creativity test. According to Yeh et al. rural children gained less than urban children probably because of weaker competencies in self-regulated learning. They suggest that creativity learning systems should be used to improve school children's creativity. The results also show the importance of self-determination and rewards in learning motivation.

Developing the child's creativity 63

Parents' role in encouraging creative thought

According to Pressey (1960), "Development of creative ability is fostered by a favourable immediate environment, warmth and affection from parents, autonomy and independence, expert instruction, frequent and progressive opportunities for the exercise of ability, social facilitation and frequent success experiences". Some methods that parents can use to stimulate their child's creativity are as follows:

- *Providing choices.* Parents must tell their children to make choices. This encourages them to think independently, exercising an important aspect of creativity.
- *Stimulation.* An environment that provides novelty and variety to the child can stimulate the child's senses and enhance creative problem-solving. Some items in the child's environment that can stimulate their imagination are drawing supplies, blocks, books and craft supplies as they can contribute to elaborate dramatic play schemes.
- Parents must *brainstorm* different uses for items with their children. For example, a cardboard tube can be a telescope or a tower. They must tell their children "what to do", not "how to do things" and also tell them to think of unusual solutions. While playing with their children, parents must use substitute items for props when needed. Such pretend play allows children to imagine life from a different perspective, an important building block of creativity.
- *Materials* that can be given to the child to encourage creativity are clay, play dough, paints, chalk, crayons, sand and water. Clay and play dough offer opportunities for children to be creative and to release energy/stress as dough can be pulled, pushed, squeezed and punched. Painting is a creative play activity as it allows children to plan, make decisions about colour and form and work on their own. Working with sand can be relaxing and it provides a smooth sensory experience. Water is an exciting and soothing play item for small children. They feel happy if they are allowed to pour and measure it, make bubbles, etc. Drawing with chalk on large areas or blank surfaces is an enjoyable activity for children.
- Parents must ask their child *open-ended questions* to stretch their understanding. They should involve the child in figuring out ways to make an improvement upon something.
- To recognize if their child is creative, parents must observe their children's method of *problem-solving* and thinking. They must find out if their child shows a tendency to question, to challenge and to change and whether they give unusual responses to questions.

Tips for teachers

- Teachers must be able to identify and encourage creative students.
- Teachers must be venturesome to handle new techniques in teaching.

64 *Child-adolescent behaviour*

- They must encourage students to ask unusual questions, to be imaginative, to think and act without their direction but within the limits of the rules.
- They must not be critical of students' work and praise them for deserving work.
- They must organize brainstorming sessions for them and give students opportunities for creative writing on unusual topics as such writing allows for free flight of imagination and creative thinking.
- According to Lucas (2001), the creative teacher should be willing to make mistakes and learn from students.

Hicks (1980) tried to determine whether the creative thinking skills of fourth-grade students could be stimulated by using classroom activities to improve fluency, flexibility and originality. Hicks' results showed that creative thinking skills can be improved by these activities. The study also found significant correlations between the child's intelligence quotient (IQ) and creativity, and between reading and creativity.

Karwowsky et al. (2020) conducted a cross-cultural study covering four countries to find out the ways in which teachers perceive creative students. They also wanted to study the similarities and differences of such perceptions among teachers from different countries. Teachers perceived creative students as showing three types of behaviour: cognitive traits, non-conformist and impulsive behaviours and adaptiveness. They found that two factors were largely equivalent in the different countries, i.e., cognitive traits associated with creativity and non-conformist and impulsive behaviours. Adaptiveness varied between countries.

The education system and creativity

The education system should try to develop in students creative problem-solving and innovative decision-making abilities. Education should train young minds both to be able to converge on one acceptable answer and also enable them to come up with a number of probable solutions to a problem. Students should be trained to weigh each solution for its practicability and appropriateness, try them singly or in different combinations in order to solve problems. According to Corazza (2016), the creative process is dynamic and, for a given creative production, creative inconclusiveness and creative achievement can alternate in time. Educational programmes should be designed for creativity and not only for creative achievement. This means that methods must be devised to build resilience against natural frustration associated with creative inconclusiveness.

Houtz et al. (1978) administered different types of creative thinking and problem-solving tasks to intellectually gifted children from second to sixth grade. They found that on creative thinking tasks, a plateau appeared in

Developing the child's creativity 65

performance from grade four, but on problem-solving tasks, growth continued until grade six. They suggest the need to train the gifted in skills of creativity and problem-solving.

Chamorro-Premuzic (2006) conducted a study on university students over four years. Students' academic performance was assessed throughout the four years through written exams, seminars (continuous assessment) and their dissertation. They found that creative thinking was more related to final dissertation marks. Exams and seminars were associated with conscientiousness rather than creative thinking. A follow-up on preferences for different assessment methods revealed that creative thinking was positively related to preference for viva-voce (oral exams), group projects and final dissertation. It was negatively associated with preferences for multiple choice and essay-type exams and continuous assessment.

Barriers to creativity

The following are some influences that make children, adolescents or adults feel hesitant to act differently. Removing these barriers and providing a supportive climate to students in the home and school/college will help to foster creative thinking.

- Peer pressure: Children may fear that they may become unpopular with their peers if their views or ideas are very different. This can lead to a decrease in creativity.
- Surveillance: Being observed by others like classmates, teachers, etc., while engaged in a creative process can undermine creativity in children.
- Strict parents/teachers: If parents or teachers are critical, dominating and disapproving in their attitude to children's behaviour, ideas, judgements and thoughts they may feel scared to think and act differently so their creative talent may be suppressed. Beloyianni and Zkainos (2021), found that students felt shy about expressing new ideas in front of students as teachers looked at it as deviant and nonconforming behaviour.
- According to Bandura (1977), children who have low self-confidence and self-efficacy or those experiencing unpleasant emotions like anger, sadness or anxiety may not try novel solutions nor want to think differently. Fear of failure is another common barrier, that is, children may avoid taking risks or trying new things out of fear of making mistakes, being criticized/not accepted by significant people.
- Having to work or submit assignments within tight deadlines can prevent the development of the child's creativity as they would tend to follow routines.

66 *Child-adolescent behaviour*

Beloyianni and Zkainos (2021) studied perceived barriers to creativity and gender differences in middle school students. They found that the most commonly prevailing barrier to creativity was lack of time and opportunities for expressing creativity. Some other barriers were shyness, inhibition and lack of motivation in students. Since there was limited social recognition and reward for creative ability, students were not motivated. There was no significant difference between genders. They concluded that schools should stimulate creative thinking in students by providing a supportive climate.

7 Learning disabilities in children

Chapter outline

- Learning
  - Meaning
  - Factors influencing learning
- Learning disabilities/disorders
  - Definition
  - Types of learning disabilities
    - Dyslexia
    - Dysgraphia
    - Preschool children
    - The school-aged child
    - The teen and young adult
  - Accommodations
    - Dyscalculia
    - DCD Dyspraxia
  - Interventions
  - Causes of learning disabilities
  - Effects of learning disabilities
  - Behavioural signs to identify learning disabilities

Learning

Meaning

According to the *APA Dictionary of Psychology* (VandenBos, 2015)

> learning is the acquisition of novel information, behaviours or abilities after practice, observation, or other experiences, as evidenced by change in behaviour, knowledge or brain function. Learning involves consciously or non-consciously attending to relevant aspects of incoming information, mentally organizing the information into a coherent cognitive representation, and integrating it with relevant existing knowledge activated from long-term memory.

DOI: 10.4324/9781003373070-7

68   *Child-adolescent behaviour*

Learning means to gain knowledge or understand a skill by study, instruction or experience. Learning is a life-long process and it helps the person to adjust to situations.

According to the theory of learning by Thorndike (1903), "learning occurs through the association between a stimulus and a response". He holds that behaviour that is followed by a positive consequence is more likely to be repeated, while behaviour that is followed by a negative consequence is less likely to be repeated.

Skinner (1968) states that learning is the process of acquiring new knowledge and new responses. He explains the difference between informal learning, which occurs naturally, and formal education, which relies on the teacher creating optimal patterns of stimulus and response (reward and punishment). He put forward the *operant conditioning theory of learning* that states that behaviour is influenced by its consequences. If a person's action is followed by a reward (reinforcement), it is likely to be learned and repeated. If an action is punished it will not be repeated by the person or will occur less frequently (Morgan and King, 1975).

Crow and Crow (1983) state that "learning is the acquisition of habits, knowledge, and attitudes".

Factors influencing learning

Learning is said to be efficient when what is learned is retained and easily recalled. There are some factors within and outside the learner that influence the rate and efficiency of the learning process. Some *internal factors*, that is, those within the learner, are the age, motivation level and intelligence of the learner, maturation, the learner's physical condition, functioning of the brain, mental health, mood, concentration and fatigue level. Some *external factors* are rewards and punishments, working conditions, length of the study period, meaningfulness of the material to be learned, the learner's home background and parental education, the teacher and teaching methods and the models with whom the learner identifies. Thus, children learn best when

- They are mature enough and ready to learn.
- When they have no physical or mental disabilities.
- When they feel confident that they can learn.
- When they have a positive mindset, as emotions influence thinking.
- When what they learn is meaningful and interesting to them.
- When they have a conducive home climate, and parental care.
- When they have suitable material and equipment and freedom to use them.
- When they have good teachers and skilful guidance.

Learning disabilities/disorders

Definition

According to Dominguez and Carungo (2023),

Learning Disabilities refer to a number of disorders that may affect the acquisition, organization, retention, comprehension or the use of both verbal and non-verbal information. Children with learning disabilities have difficulty learning, but they have average or above average intelligence quotient.

According to Hammill et al. (1981), "Learning disability is a generic term that refers to a heterogeneous group of disorders manifested by significant difficulties in the acquisition or use of listening, speaking, reading, writing, reasoning or mathematical abilities".

According to the APA DSM-5 (2013)

Specific learning disorders often referred to as learning disorder or learning disability are neurodevelopmental disorders that are typically diagnosed in early school-aged children, although may not be recognized until adulthood. They are characterized by a persistent impairment in at least one of three major areas: reading, writing, arithmetic or mathematical reasoning skills during formal years of schooling. They are categorized as mild, moderate, and severe. Symptoms might include:

Inaccurate or slow and effortful reading, poor written expression that lacks clarity, difficulties remembering number facts, or inaccurate mathematical reasoning.

Current academic skills must be well below the average range of scores in culturally and linguistically appropriate tests of reading, writing or maths.

The individual's difficulties must not be better explained by developmental, neurological, sensory (vision or hearing) or motor disorders and must significantly interfere with academic achievement, occupational performance, or activities of daily living.

According to the *APA Dictionary of Psychology* (Vandebos, 2015)

learning disabilities include learning problems that result from perceptual disabilities, brain injury and minimal brain dysfunction but exclude those that result from visual impairment or hearing loss; intellectual disability; emotional disturbance; or environmental, cultural or economic factors. For diagnostic purposes, learning disability is the condition that exists when a

70 *Child-adolescent behaviour*

person's actual performance on achievement tests in reading, mathematics or written expression is substantially (typically two standard deviations) below that expected for his or her established intelligence, age, and grade.

According to Rimrodt and Lipkin (2011), "learning disability represents a disability based on a discrepancy between a person's overall intellectual ability and actual academic performance".

Types of learning disabilities

The three types of learning disabilities are merged into one diagnostic category under "Special Learning Disabilities" (SLD) in the DSM-5-TR (2022). To identify the area of academic weakness the three different specifiers are: (1) with impairment in reading – dyslexia, (2) with impairment in writing – dysgraphia and (3) with impairment in mathematics – dyscalculia. The different types of learning disabilities are as follows.

Dyslexia

Dyslexia is a learning disability that involves difficulty in reading. According to the International Dyslexia Association (2002), "Dyslexia refers to difficulties with accurate and/or fluent word recognition, poor spelling and deficits in coding abilities". According to Dominguez and Carungo (2023),

> Reading disability is the most common learning disability representing 80% of all learning disabilities and males outnumber females. It results from deficits in phonological processing. Skills necessary for appropriate phonological processing involve reading, decoding, phonics, ability to produce sounds and proper auditory capabilities. The progression often originates with problems in reading and decoding in the more nascent years, on to dysfluent reading, and then to difficulty in reading comprehension. The child may want to avoid reading altogether.

According to APA DSM-5-TR (2022),

> dyslexia means the person demonstrates significant impairment in one or more of the reading subskills including, word reading accuracy, reading rate or fluency, and/or reading comprehension. The person may have problems with decoding and spelling. Children with dyslexia may have trouble with breaking down spoken words into syllables and/or recognizing words that rhyme. They may also find it difficult to connect letters they see on a page with the sounds they make. As a result, reading becomes slow and effortful and not a fluent process. They may also have difficulty with writing accuracy and spelling.

Learning disabilities in children 71

Bosse et al. (2007) studied children with dyslexia and found that both visual attention deficits and a phonological disorder can be associated with dyslexia causing reading problems for different reasons. According to Bosse et al., the visual attention (VA) span might contribute to developmental dyslexia independent of a phonological disorder. VA span is defined as the amount of distinct visual elements that can be processed in parallel in a multi-element array.

According to Snowling et al. (2020b),

dyslexia is used to describe children who experience problems learning to read and write; and who have persistent problems with reading fluency and learning, often when a basic level of reading fluency and spelling ability is established. They are slow to learn to decode words and become fluent, they find it difficult to generalise, that is, to read novel words they have not read before. They describe phonological awareness as the most underlying problem in developmental dyslexia. To diagnose dyslexia in a child, the decoding and spelling fluency problems should be evident from early school years and should persist over time. It should affect the child's academic functioning. The diagnosis may be mild, moderate or severe.

According to Snowling et al. (2020b), problems with literacy may continue up to adulthood and are associated with lower levels of educational attainment, higher rates of unskilled employment and often periods of unemployment. *Comorbidities* refer to the co-occurrence of two or more disorders in the same individual. Dyslexia has been found to be comorbid with

- Maths disorder.
- Attentional and motor coordination problems.
- Speech sound disorder.
- Socio-emotional and behaviour disorders.
- Internalizing problems like anxiety and depression.
- Oral language problems or developmental language disorders (DLD).
- Dysgraphia.

Snowling et al. (2020a) found that DLD, a communication disorder, is a major risk factor for dyslexia. The results of their study were that children with dyslexia and DLDs have reading comprehension difficulties because of weak decoding in the case of dyslexia and weak oral language skills in the case of DLD. According to Landerl and Moll (2010), dyscalculia is frequently comorbid with dyslexia in 30 per cent to 70 per cent of cases as both reading and mathematics are complex skills with multiple components.

72 *Child-adolescent behaviour*

Dysgraphia

Dysgraphia is a learning disability where the child exhibits difficulties with writing, that is, physically writing words legibly and quickly, to issues with organizing and expressing thought in written form. According to Chung et al. (2020),

> writing is an important and complex task that typically develops in early childhood. Dysgraphia is a learning disorder in which the person shows problems with letter formation/legibility, letter spacing, spelling, fine motor co-ordination, rate of writing, grammar and composition. The individual's writing skills are below the level expected for his or her age and cognitive level. Dysgraphia can occur alone or in children who also have dyslexia, other learning disorders, Attention Deficit Hyperactivity Disorder (ADHD), cerebral palsy or autism spectrum disorder.

According to the APA DSM-5-TR (2022), children with dysgraphia show impaired spelling and problems with writing that can include difficulties with accuracy, grammar and punctuation and/or clarity or organization of written expression. The child may have trouble breaking down spoken words into syllables and recognizing words that rhyme. The child has difficulties putting their thoughts on paper. Kindergarten-age children with problems in written expression may not be able to recognize and write letters as well as their peers. According to the *APA Dictionary of Psychology* (VandenBos, 2015)

> Dysgraphia or agraphia is loss or impairment of the ability to write as a result of neurological damage or disorder. The specific forms of writing difficulties vary considerably but may include problems with spelling irregular or ambiguous words, writing numbers or particular letters or performing the motor movements needed for handwriting.

According to the United States National Center for Learning Disabilities (Chung et al., 2020), the signs of dysgraphia at different age levels are as follows.

PRESCHOOL CHILDREN

- An awkward grip or body position when writing.
- Tire easily with writing.
- Avoidance of writing and drawing tasks.
- Written letters are poorly formed, inversed, reversed or inconsistently spaced, difficulty staying within margins.

Learning disabilities in children 73

THE SCHOOL-AGED CHILD

- Illegible handwriting.
- Switching between cursive and print.
- Difficulty with word-finding, sentence completion and written comprehension.

THE TEENAGER AND YOUNG ADULT

- Difficulty with written organization of thought.
- Difficulty with written syntax and written grammar that is not duplicated with oral tasks.

Dohla et al. (2018) assessed spelling and reading abilities in third- and fourth-grade children. Their results showed that phonological processing abilities, auditory skills and visual magnocellular functions affected spelling ability.

Accommodations

According to Chung et al. (2020),

accommodations should be directed to decrease the stress associated with writing. Specific devices may be utilized, such as larger pencils with special grips and paper with raised lines to provide tactile feedback. Extra time should be permitted for class assignments, homework, tests, quizzes. Depending on the students' comfort level, alternative ways of demonstrating knowledge like oral responses rather than written exam should be considered. Handwriting practice should continue at school as written language is needed for many daily tasks.

Dyscalculia

Dyscalculia refers to a learning disability in mathematics. According to the APA DSM-5 (2013), dyscalculia is a term used to describe difficulties in learning number-related concepts or using symbols and functions to perform maths calculations. Problems with maths can include difficulties with number sense, memorizing maths facts and maths calculation. The child demonstrates significantly below-average skills in number sense, memorization of arithmetic facts, accurate or fluent calculation and/or accurate math reasoning. According to the *APA Dictionary of Psychology* (VandenBos, 2015),

Dyscalculia is an impaired ability to perform simple arithmetic operations that result from congenital defect. It is a developmental condition...

74 Child-adolescent behaviour

Acalculia is the loss of the ability to perform simple arithmetic operations that result from brain injury or disease usually to the parietal lobe. It is an acquired condition

According to Dominguez and Carungo (2023),

dyscalculia is a weakness in performing mathematical operations. The person will experience impediments, organizing problems, finishing multiple step calculations, distinguishing math calculation signs. Proper math sense is incumbent on neurodevelopmental functions like number sense, calculation and retrieval of math facts, the language of math, visual-spatial skills and comprehension of word problems.

Soares et al. (2018) state that dyscalculia is a neurodevelopmental disorder involving dysfunction in specific brain regions that are implicated in maths skills. Certain genetic conditions increase the risk of a child having dyscalculia.

According to Gobel and Snowling (2010), dyscalculia and dyslexia are comorbid because many aspects of mathematics depend on verbal skills, for example, number knowledge, counting, retrieval of number facts and verbal problem-solving. Basic number processing in adults with dyscalculia is intact. Their difficulties are restricted to the verbal code and are not associated with deficits in non-verbal magnitude representation, visual Arabic number form or spatial recognition. Kucian et al. (2018) investigated if there is a connection between mathematics anxiety, negative emotions, low performance and deficiencies in mathematics abilities in children between seven and eleven years with developmental dyscalculia. Their findings were that:

- All children were faster and made fewer errors in addition than in subtraction.
- Children with developmental dyslexia showed higher levels of mathematics anxiety.
- There were no gender differences in maths anxiety.
- Children with maths anxiety performed worse in maths-related topics (mathematical performance, arithmetic fluency, addition, subtraction, number line performance) and in working memory.

According to Soares et al. (2018), "Math anxiety" is specific to maths and is a negative emotional reaction or a state of discomfort involving maths tasks. Children with maths anxiety can develop a negative attitude to maths in general, avoidance of maths activities and anxious feelings. Poor maths achievement is strongly related to maths anxiety. To help children with problems in maths tasks, Soares et al. suggest some methods as follows:

Learning disabilities in children 75

- Behavioural interventions like cognitive behaviour therapy (CBT) and systematic desensitization.
- Improving the child's attention level.
- Tutorials to improve basic maths knowledge and skills.
- Technologies like computers and tablets with touchscreens as they can be used with few instructions.

According to Butterworth (2005), development of arithmetical abilities can be described in terms of "numerosity", which refers to the number of objects in a set, and increasing skill in manipulating numerosities. The child's concept of numerosity appears to be innate. The impairment in the capacity to learn arithmetic is interpreted in many cases as a deficit in the child's concept of numerosity.

Developmental coordination disorder (dyspraxia)

According to the APA DSM-5 (2013), "Developmental Coordination Disorder (DCD) is a neurodevelopmental disorder with primary deficits in fine and gross motor coordination". The DSM-5 criteria for DCD diagnosis include:

1. The acquisition and execution of motor skills and related coordination are below what is expected based on age, for example, the person may have taken longer to learn to walk, write, etc. They may have learned motor skills but struggled to execute them in a coordinated fashion.
2. The deficits of motor skill and coordination significantly interfere with daily life in the domains of self-care, scholastics, work, leisure and play. For example, the individual may avoid team sports in fear of embarrassment for lack of coordination. The child might have difficulties in fine motor tasks such as trouble gripping objects, poor handwriting and challenges typing on a keyboard. Difficulties might involve gross motor functions such as frequently tripping over or bumping into objects, difficulties in catching or kicking a ball or trouble walking in a coordinated manner.
3. The symptoms begin in childhood.
4. The deficits cannot be better explained by any other condition, for example, the person should not have cerebral palsy, brain injury, neurodegenerative disorders or difficulties related to surgery, etc.

According to Castelliocci and Singla (2024),

DCD is a neurodevelopmental disorder characterized by poor motor coordination and difficulty in learning motor skills. It affects the child's

76 *Child-adolescent behaviour*

academic performance and interferes with his/her socialization. It may result in executive function deficits and prevent effective learning. The child may find it difficult to execute motor actions accurately, his/her movements may be slow and he/she has handwriting problems. Children with DCD write fewer words per minute than children without DCD.

They further state that Van Galen's model analyzes handwriting difficulties in DCD by integrating cognitive, linguistic and biomechanical aspects of handwriting. There are three *premotor stages* that have an impact on the child's handwriting speed (the number of words produced per minute):

1. This stage requires the writer to be motivated and this activates the child's intention to write.
2. This is the semantic retrieval stage and here the writer develops ideas from vocabulary.
3. In this stage the writer elaborates on what to write and retrieves semantic information before initiating the motor writing task on paper.

Next is the phase of *motor planning*, that is, matching the phoneme or letter's sound with the grapheme or the symbol. Children with DCD have significant difficulty with words composed of two or more syllables.

The last stage is that of *muscular adjustment* and here the signal travels from the brain to the hand. Of the population of children with DCD, 95 per cent have handwriting problems, with 57 per cent demonstrating decreased legibility, writing speed and letter formation quality compared to their peers.

Farmer et al. (2017) say that DCD is the sum of fine motor, perceptual, visual and executive difficulties that emerge during childhood brain development and last throughout adulthood. It sometimes mimics other developmental disorders like ADHD or intellectual deficiency.

According to Pranjic et al. (2023), attention deficit hyperactivity disorder (ADHD) and DCD co-occur in approximately 50 per cent of the cases.

Interventions

Meachon et al. (2022) state that the

possible causes of DCD are low birth weight and premature births, particularly among males. An interdisciplinary approach along with occupational therapists and physiotherapists can help children to improve their motor skills and coordination. Psychological support is also important to reduce emotional reactions like anxiety or depression. Specific difficulties and goals of the person are considered while using coping strategies.

Learning disabilities in children 77

Causes of learning disabilities

According to Hammill et al. (1981), learning disabilities are intrinsic to the individual and are presumed to be due to central nervous system dysfunction. They may occur concomitantly with other conditions (e.g., sensory disability) or environmental influences (inappropriate instruction, cultural differences); however, it is not the direct result of those conditions or influences. One cause of learning disabilities is variation in the child's brain structure and function that impact the basic psychological processes involved in learning. Premature babies are more likely than full-term babies to have learning problems later on in life. A child is more likely to have a learning disability if their parent or sibling has a learning disability.

Effects of learning disabilities

According to Arsovski et al. (2023), learning disabilities can affect a child's academic performance, social relationships, overall well-being, emotional development and also cause low self-respect and stress in the child. They may dislike going to school. With early identification and intervention, children with learning disabilities can become skilled learners and they may be able to build on their strengths.

According to Rimrodt and Lipkin (2011), if learning disabilities are not identified and addressed at an early stage the student may resort to protective mechanisms to minimize damage to their self-esteem. Early signs of learning disabilities may help in early identification. Rimrodt and Lipkin state that some signs of learning disabilities are as follows:

- If the child has a history of preschool developmental problems, it can indicate that the child has an increased risk for learning disabilities and educational difficulties.
- The child is premature or has a family history of learning disability and educational difficulties.
- A child with a a preschool speech and language disorder may later experience educational difficulties in areas such as comprehension of language-based instruction or phonemic process used in the development of early word reading or decoding.
- Difficulties with recognition and drawing of shapes in preschool may indicate problems in letter recognition or writing.
- Such language and visual-motor difficulties may be associated with problems with the sound/symbol associations needed for reading.

Rimrodt and Lipkin (2011) list some signs and symptoms of learning disabilities and school failure. They are:

78 *Child-adolescent behaviour*

- Increased learning effort – school is boring for the child, they have school anxiety, they may show class-clown behaviour and spend much longer completing homework than classmates.
- School distress – frequent failing grades, frequent absences, social disengagement, frequent detention, suspensions, aggression and bullying behaviours.
- School failure – retention, expulsion, dropping out.

Diagnosis and Interventions: According to the APA DSM-5 (2013), early identification is important so that intervention can begin early. Children will not have to go through school-related problems and psychological stress. Education for a child with a learning disability may make use of multimodal teaching, that is, using multiple senses. According to Dominguez and Carungo (2023), the diagnosis and management of children with learning disabilities involves the coordination of a team of professionals who specialize in particular domains such as speech and language therapists, occupational therapists, clinical psychologists, physicians and those trained in special education. Some specific educational strategies in managing children with learning disabilities are increasing phonological awareness, remediating letter-sound proficiency in children with dyslexia, and reading aloud repeatedly to improve fluency. Children with dysgraphia are taught hand-eye exercises. Children with dyscalculia are made to practise number syntax.

According to the APA DSM-5-TR (2022), students with learning disabilities often benefit from accommodations such as additional time on tests and written assignments, using computers for typing rather than writing by hand and smaller class size. Successful strategies and intervention for a child may change over time as the child develops. Special education services can help children with learning disabilities to improve their reading, writing and maths skills. Effective interventions involve systematic, intensive and individualized instruction that may improve the learning difficulties and/or help the individual to use strategies to compensate for the disorder. The most effective method to help children with reading difficulties are structured and targeted strategies that address phonological awareness, decoding skills, comprehension and fluency. Coping strategies for writing problems are in two general areas: the process of writing and of composing written expression. Children with dyscalculia are given multisensory instruction to understand math concepts. Accompaniments like using manipulative and assistive technology may also help children with dyscalculia.

According to Arsovski et al. (2023), occupational therapy is effective in addressing the needs of children with learning disabilities. Occupational therapists assess a child's cognitive, sensory, motor and emotional functions and use strategies based on the individual's needs. These include methods to improve motor skills, sensory integration techniques and cognitive exercises to improve mental functions like concentration or organization. Occupational

Learning disabilities in children 79

therapists also train children with learning disabilities in life skills and try to increase their self-esteem and foster overall independence.

Behavioural signs to identify learning disabilities

- If the child shows a significant delay in achieving milestones for walking and talking, it may indicate a learning problem.
- If the child does not develop age-appropriate speech and language skills.
- If the child has difficulties with fine motor tasks like buttoning a shirt or tying shoelaces, they are likely to have problems in handwriting.
- The child has a weak memory and cannot concentrate on any given task for more than a few minutes, or they cannot remember two or more instructions in sequence.
- The child cannot hold the chalk properly.
- The child's reading is slow and laboured and they do not like reading.
- The child performs well on oral tasks but when it comes to reading or written assignments there is a considerable dip in performance.
- The child finds copying from the blackboard an arduous task and does not complete written work on time.
- The child uses spoonerisms such as "par cark" for "car park" and has difficulty remembering nursery rhymes.
- The child has trouble with organization of numbers or has trouble with counting principles.

8 Behavioural/emotional disorders in children

Chapter outline

- Meaning of behaviour disorders
  - Signs
- Preventive measures
- Types of behaviour disorders
  - Attention deficit hyperactivity disorder
    - Inattention
    - Hyperactivity
    - Impulsivity
    - Causes of ADHD
  - Anxiety disorders
    - Types of anxiety disorder
    - Interventions
  - Disruptive behaviour disorders
  - Oppositional defiant disorder
    - Conduct Disorder
    - Interventions
  - Aggression in children
    - Characteristics of aggressive behaviours
    - Risk factors
    - Interventions
  - Stuttering
    - Symptoms
    - Causes
    - Interventions

Meaning of behaviour disorders

According to Ogundele (2018), some common mental health disorders (MHD) in pre-school and school age children include emotional and behavioural disorders (EBD) such as:

DOI: 10.4324/9781003373070-8

Behavioural/emotional disorders in children 81

- Disruptive behaviour problems: attention deficit hyperactivity disorder, conduct disorder (CD), oppositional defiant disorder (ODD) and temper tantrums
- Emotional problems: Obsessive compulsive disorders (OCD), anxiety, depression.
- Developmental disorders: Speech and language delay, intellectual disability.
- Pervasive disorders: Autism spectrum disorder.

He classifies emotional and behavioural problems (EBP) or disorders (EBD) as either "internalising" (emotional disorders like depression and anxiety) or "externalising" (disruptive behaviours such as ADHD and CD).

Ogundale states that

> While low-intensity, naughty, defiant and impusive behaviour from time-to-time, losing one's temper, destruction of property, and deceitfulness/ stealing in the preschool children are regarded as normal, extremely difficult and challenging behaviours outside the norm for the age and level of development, such as unpredictable, prolonged, and/or destructive tantrums and severe outbursts of temper loss are recognized as behaviour disorders. Community studies have identified that more than 80% of pre-schoolers have mild tantrums sometimes but a smaller proportion, less than 10% will have daily tantrums, regarded as normative misbehaviours at this age. Challenging behaviours and emotional difficulties are more likely to be recognized as "problems" rather than "disorders" during the first 2 years of life. Emotional problems, such as anxiety, depression and post-traumatic stress disorder (PTSD) tend to occur in later childhood.

Ogundale further states that behavioural and emotional problems that occur in childhood can have negative impacts on the individual, the family and the society.

A behaviour disorder in a child is a problematic behaviour that is severe, persists for a long time and does not conform to the expected behaviour of a child for their age. The *causes* could be constitutional, emotional, environmental or a combination of these factors. Constitutional causes include intellectual disability, brain injury, endocrine imbalance, obesity or physical disability in the child.

Signs

Some persistent behaviours displayed by children that can be signs of behaviour problems are: Nail-biting, thumb-sucking, bed-wetting, faecal-soiling, frequent crying, crying easily, over-timidity (shyness), nervousness, stealing, cheating, cruelty, aggression and destruction, extreme sensitivity,

82 Child-adolescent behaviour

persistent inattentiveness, twisting and pulling of hair, continuous lies, temper tantrums, refusing to follow rules, questioning authority and difficulty handling anger.

Preventive measures

The first five years are the most important years in a child's life. The mental and emotional growth of the child is largely dependent on the social interactions, anxieties and gratifications that occur in these five years. So, educating parents about having proper attitudes towards the child is required. The provision of a congenial atmosphere in school and recreational facilities is important. Early identification of children with cerebral palsy, intellectual disability or physical disability is essential so that interventions and coping strategies can be applied.

Types of behaviour disorders

Attention deficit hyperactivity disorder

According to Wolraich et al. (2019),

ADHD is a common neuro-behavioural disorder of childhood and symptoms sometimes continue in adolescence and adulthood. It can affect the child's academic achievement, mental health and social interactions. Boys are more than twice as likely as girls to be diagnosed with ADHD.

According to the APA's *Diagnostic and Statistical Manual of Mental Disorders* (2013) Fifth Edition (DSM-5),

ADHD is a neuro-developmental disorder defined by impairing levels of inattention, disorganization, and/or hyperactivity-impulsivity. Inattention and disorganization entail inability to stay on task, seeming not to listen, and losing materials necessary for task at levels that are inconsistent with age or developmental level. Hyperactivity-impulsivity entails over activity, fidgeting, inability to stay seated, intruding into other people's activities, and inability to wait – symptoms that are excessive for age or developmental level.

Children with ADHD can be hyperactive, impulsive and inattentive (they can have difficulty focusing and maintaining attention). A study byCunningham et al. (2002) found that teachers reported problems , like more social behaviour, classroom management and internalizing problems in children at risk for ADHD, compared to children who were not at risk for ADHD. Behere et al.

Behavioural/emotional disorders in children 83

(2017) found that children with only one parent due to death or divorce were more likely to have an ADHD diagnosis.

The APA's DSM-5 (2013) distinguishes between three *subtypes* of ADHD, as follows:

- Children who are predominantly inattentive.
- Children who are predominantly hyperactive/impulsive.
- Children who show a mix of these two types of symptoms.

If the child/adolescent shows a persistent pattern of inattention, hyperactivity and impulsivity that interferes with normal functioning for at least six months, they are diagnosed as having ADHD disorder.

Inattention: Six or more of the following symptoms should have persisted for at least six months to a degree that is inconsistent with the child's developmental level and that negatively impacts directly on the child's social and academic/occupational activities.

- Often do not pay close attention to details/they make careless mistakes in schoolwork.
- Often have difficulties sustaining attention in tasks or play activities.
- Often do not listen, even when spoken to directly.
- Often easily distracted by extraneous stimuli.
- Often do not follow instructions and fail to finish schoolwork.
- Often avoid/dislike doing school work or doing tasks that require focused mental effort.
- Often has difficulty organizing tasks and activities.
- Often lose items needed for school activities like books, pens, assignments, etc.
- Often forgetful in daily activities like doing chores.

Hyperactivity and impulsivity: Six or more of the following symptoms should have persisted for at least six months to a degree that is inconsistent with the child's developmental level and negatively impacts directly on the child's social and academic/occupational activities.

Hyperactivity

- They have difficulty staying seated in the classroom or in other situations where being seated is expected.
- Often fidget with books or pencils, tap hands and feet or squirm in the seat.
- Often run around, climb in situations where it is inappropriate.
- They talk too much/keep asking questions.

84 *Child-adolescent behaviour*

- Often unable to play or take part in leisure activities quietly.
- Is often "on the go" acting as if "driven by a motor".

Impulsivity

- Often interrupt others' conversations, games or activities or intrudes on others.
- They have trouble waiting for their turn, for example, while waiting in line.
- Often blurt out an answer before a question has been completed.

Causes of ADHD

Genetics contributes to ADHD, but no specific gene has been identified as a cause. Some non-genetic factors that have been linked are low birth weight, premature birth, exposure to toxins like alcohol and/or lead during pregnancy and extreme stress during pregnancy (Elmaghraby and Garayalde, 2002).

Interventions for ADHD: According to Wolraich et al. (2019), for preschool-aged children between four and six years, parent training in behaviour management (PTBM) and/or behavioural classroom interventions should be used. If there is no significant improvement, medication may be considered after weighing the risks involved. For children between six and twelve years of age they recommend medication and PTBM and/or behavioural classroom intervention. For adolescents between twelve and eighteen years, medicines should first be given and training interventions or behavioural interventions should be used. Educational interventions include the school environment, class placement and behavioural supports. Parent–child interaction therapy is one example of PTBM. Behavioural therapy involves training parents and teachers to respond to children's and adolescents' behaviours such as interrupting, aggression or not completing tasks.

Anxiety disorders

The perception of specific danger arouses fear in children. The child knows what they are afraid of. Anxiety is a vague sense of fear/uneasiness in which the cause of the anxiety is not clear to the child. According to Freud, the father of mental health and psychoanalysis, "anxiety is a painful emotion which acts as a signal of impending danger to the ego. The person tries to overcome this anxiety using defence mechanisms" (Pervin, 1980).

The APA's DSM-5 (2013) defines anxiety as "Excessive anxiety and worry (apprehensive expectation) occurring more days than not for at least six months, about a number of events or activities (such as work or school

Behavioural/emotional disorders in children 85

performance). The person finds it difficult to control the anxiety". According to the APA, some symptoms of anxiety are:

- Feelings of being on edge or restlessness.
- Tiring easily or more fatigued than usual.
- Impaired concentration or feeling as though the mind goes blank.
- Irritability (which may or may not be observable to others).
- Increased muscle aches or soreness.

Anxiety is both a mental and physical state of negative expectation. Mentally, it can make the person aroused and worried. Physically, it affects various body systems like the digestive system, sleep, heart rate, etc. Children express fear and anxiety towards some animals, insects, people, places, objects, situations, the dark, loud noises and ghosts. According to the National Institute of Mental Health (2024), occasional anxiety is a normal part of life, an emotion that people experience. However, an anxiety disorder means that the anxiety does not go away, it is more than temporary worry, and gets worse over time. The symptoms interfere with the person's day-to-day activities such as the child's performance in school, relationships and job performance.

Types of anxiety disorder

According to the APA DSM-5 (Stein et al., 2014), each anxiety disorder is characterized by excessive fear and anxiety as well as related behavioural disturbances, including avoidance symptoms. Anxiety disorders differ from one another in that each has a different mean age of onset, symptoms are precipitated by different situations or objects and most are characterized by cognitive ideation that differs across disorders.

According to the APA DSM-5 (Stein et al., 2014), the symptoms, emotions and behaviours experienced by the person in each anxiety disorder are as follows:

- *Separation anxiety disorder (SAD)*. According to Stein et al. (2014), a child with SAD shows recurrent excessive distress with actual or anticipated separation from home or attachment figure(s); persistent and pervasive worry about losing the attachment figure(s) or possible harm befalling them, such as illness, injury, disasters or death". Adults may also experience SAD, that is, fear of being away from people whom they are close to. They avoid being alone and may feel unwell when separation is about to happen.
- *Selective mutism.*Stein et al.(2014) state that, selective mutism means consistent failure to speak in specific social situations (in which there is an expectation for speaking, e.g., at school) despite speaking in other situations (e.g., at home). The disturbance interferes with educational or

86 *Child-adolescent behaviour*

occupational achievement or with social communication. The duration of the disturbance is at least one month (not limited to the first month of school). The failure to speak is not attributable to a lack of knowledge of, or comfort with, the spoken language required in the social situation. The disturbance is not better explained by a communication disorder (e.g., childhood-onset-fluency disorder) and does not occur exclusively during the course of autism spectrum disorder, schizophrenia, or another psychotic disorder.

- *Generalized anxiety disorder (GAD).* Stein et al.(2014) state that GAD is characterized by excessive anxiety and worry (apprehensive expectation), occurring more days than not for at least six months, about a number of events or activities (such as work or school performance). The person finds it difficult to control the worry. The anxiety or worry are associated with three or more of the following six symptoms present for more days than not for the past six months.
  - Restlessness or feeling keyed-up or on-edge.
  - Being easily fatigued.
  - Difficulty concentrating or mind going blank.
  - Irritability.
  - Muscle tension.
  - Sleep disturbances (difficulty falling or staying asleep, or restless unsatisfactory sleep).
- *Social anxiety disorder (social phobia).* According to Stein et al.(2014), social anxiety disorder is defined as, a marked or persistent fear of one or more social or performance situations in which the person is exposed to unfamiliar people or to possible scrutiny by others. The individual fears that he or she will act in a way (or show anxiety symptoms) that will be humiliating or embarrassing. The following are the criteria of social anxiety disorders:
  - Persistent, intense fear or anxiety about specific social situations because you may be judged negatively, embarrassed or humiliated.
  - Avoidance of anxiety-producing social situations or enduring them with intense fear or anxiety.
  - Difficulty making eye contact with people they do not know, speaking very softly, blushing, sweating, trembling, racing heart, stomach ache.
- *Panic disorder.* According to Stein et al.(2014), a panic disorder is an anxiety disorder characterized by repeated panic attacks. Panic attacks refer to sudden onset of fear or distress that reaches a peak in minutes. The person may experience symptoms like chest pain, racing heart, choking sensations, giddiness, nausea, hot flushes, chills, trembling, shortness of breath, unsteadiness, gastrointestinal problems and fear of dying. Often there is no specific trigger to the attack.

Behavioural/emotional disorders in children 87

- *Agoraphobia.* According to Stein et al (2014), agoraphobia means the person experiences fear or anxiety about and/or avoidance of situations where help may not be available or where it may be difficult to leave the situation if things go wrong. For example, fear of open places/enclosed places or crowds or standing in a line or being outside home alone.
- *Substance/medication-induced anxiety disorder.*According to Stein et al. (2014), substance/medication-induced anxiety disorder is a mental health condition characterized by nervousness, restlessness or panic that is directly caused by the use/abuse or withdrawal of a substance or a medication. This disorder can result from various substances, including alcohol, drugs, prescription medications, or exposure to toxins.
- *According to Stein et al.(2014), anxiety disorder due to another medical condition* includes symptoms of intense anxiety or panic that are directly caused by a physical health problem.
- *According to Stein et al.(2014), other specified anxiety disorders and unspecified anxiety disorder*s are terms for anxiety or phobias that do not meet the exact criteria for any other anxiety disorder but are significant enough to be disturbing and disruptive.
- *Specific phobias.* According to Stein et al. (2014), specific phobias refer to an anxiety disorder formerly called simple phobia. It is characterized by a marked and persistent fear about a specific object or situation or activity (e.g., dogs, blood, flying, heights). The phobic object or situation almost always provokes immediate fear or anxiety which may take the form of a panic attack. In children, the anxiety may be expressed by crying, tantrums, freezing or clinging. The fear or anxiety is out of proportion to the actual danger posed by the specific object or situation and socio-cultural context. The phobic situation is avoided or else is endured with anxiety or distress. The avoidance, anxious anticipation or distress during the feared situations interferes significantly with the person's normal routine, work (or school) functioning or social activities or relationships. There is marked distress about having the phobia. The fear is persistent, typically lasting for at least six months. The anxiety, panic attacks or avoidance associated with the specific object or situation are not better accounted for by another mental disorder such as obsessive-compulsive disorder, post-traumatic stress disorder, SAD, social phobia, panic disorder etc.

According to the APA *Dictionary of Psychology* (Vanden Bos, 2015), specific phobias are classified into five sub-types:
- Animal sub-type, which includes fears of animals or insects (e.g., cats, dogs, birds, mice, ants, snakes).
- Natural environment type, which includes fears of entities in the natural surroundings (e.g., heights, storms, water, lightning).

88 Child-adolescent behaviour

- Blood-injection-injury type, which includes fears of seeing blood or an injury or of receiving an injection or other invasive medical procedures.
- Situational type, which includes fear of public transportation, elevators, bridges, driving, flying, enclosed places (claustrophobia) and so forth.
- Other type, which includes fears that cannot be classified under any of the other sub-types (e.g., fears of choking, vomiting or contracting an illness; children's fears of clowns or loud noises).

Some common phobias are given below:

- *Acrophobia*: Fear of heights.
- *Claustrophobia*: Fear of closed spaces.
- *Pyrophobia*: Fear of fire.
- *Aquaphobia*: Fear of water.
- *Arachnophobia*: Fear of spiders.
- *Haemophobia*: Fear of blood.
- *Agoraphobia*: Fear of open places.
- *School phobia*: Fear of school.
- *Pogonophobia*: Fear of beards.
- *Cynophobia*: Fear of dogs.

Bitner et al. (2007) found that anxiety disorders in childhood are predictors of a range of psychiatric disorders in adolescence like SAD, over anxious disorder (OAD), GAD and social phobia. Alfano et al. (2007) found that 88 per cent of youth (child/adolescent) with anxiety disorders (generalized anxiety, separation anxiety or social anxiety/social phobia) experienced sleep-related problems.

According to the National Institute of Mental Health (2024), the *risk factors* for developing anxiety disorders could be genetic and or environmental. Some risk factors are shyness or feeling disturbed or nervous in new situations in childhood, exposure to stressful life events or environmental events, and history of anxiety or other mental health conditions in biological relatives. Anxiety symptoms can be produced or aggravated by physical health conditions like thyroid problem or heart arrhythmia, caffeine or other substances or medications.

Interventions

According to the National Institute of Mental Health (2024), interventions for anxiety disorders include psychotherapy (talk therapy) and/or medications. Cognitive behaviour therapy (CBT), exposure therapy and acceptance and

Behavioural/emotional disorders in children 89

commitment therapy are used. CBT teaches people different ways of thinking and reacting to situations to help them to feel less anxious and fearful. Exposure therapy focuses on making the person confront their fears and engage in activities that they have been avoiding. It is sometimes used with relaxation exercises. Acceptance and commitment therapy use strategies such as mindfulness, meditation and goal-setting to reduce anxiety. Medications are sometimes used with psychotherapy to reduce symptoms.

Parents can display some behaviours to help the child to cope with phobias and anxieties:

- They should not be too strict or punitive with children and should allow children to be adventurous. According to Devi (2014), if parents are very strict and use corporal punishment, the child may show emotional reactions like fear, anxiety, reduced confidence and avoidance of the parent.
- Parents must make themselves a model by showing appropriate expressions and actions like being calm in fear or anxiety arousing situations because children learn a lot by imitation and identification (Bandura, 1977).
- They should spend adequate time with children and praise them on their accomplishments, since this makes them feel secure.
- They must encourage drawing, painting, music and other artistic expression in their children and should also encourage them to talk about their fears because it helps them to vent their feelings.
- The parent can suggest ways for the child to cope with the fear, like taking slow breaths. They can also teach the child to repeat fear-reducing statements and positive assertions like "I can do it", "It is not as difficult as I thought" or giving them physical support.
- Seeing some images from movies/television/internet or reading ghost stories can trigger fear in children. Parents must observe whether their child's reading material or media exposure is the source of their fear.

Disruptive behaviour disorders

Conduct disorder and oppositional defiant disorder (ODD) are called disruptive behaviour disorders.

- *Oppositional defiant disorder* is defined in the APA DSM-5 (2013) as "A pattern of angry/irritable mood, argumentative/defiant behaviour, or vindictiveness". This behaviour is usually expressed towards peers, parents, teachers and other authority figures. For a child to be diagnosed with ODD, they must exhibit at least four out of eight symptoms found in the diagnostic criteria (APA DSM-5, 2013) for at least six months. A child with ODD may argue frequently with adults, show anger towards

90 *Child-adolescent behaviour*

authoritative figures, especially parents and teachers, and they may be spiteful and annoying on purpose. They can be defiant, disobedient, negativistic, short-tempered and refuse to follow rules at school and in their home. In many cases, particularly without early diagnosis, these symptoms may worsen over time, sometimes becoming severe enough to eventually lead to a diagnosis of conduct disorder.

The possible risk factors for ODD are:

- The child's temperament, that is, a child who cannot manage their emotions and has low frustration tolerance.
- Children with ADHD display oppositional behaviours at times. According to Campbell, "hyperactive/inattentive behaviours may increase the child's risk of becoming involved in negative parent-child exchanges and coercive family interactions which are associated with the development of oppositional and aggressive behaviours" (Stormshak and Bierman, 1998).
- Overly strict parents, neglect by parents, having parents with substance use disorder or inconsistent discipline by parents or teachers.

Cunnigham et al. (2002) found that mothers of children at risk for ODD reported more family dysfunction, felt less competent as parents and had higher depression scores than mothers of children without ODD symptoms.

Conduct disorder

Conduct disorder is a more extreme condition than ODD. The APA DSM-5 (2013) diagnosis of conduct disorder is,

> typically assigned to individuals under age eighteen, who habitually violate the rights of others, and will not conform their behaviour to the law or social norms appropriate for their age. It may also be described as juvenile delinquency.

A child is said to have a conduct disorder if they repeatedly exhibit aggressive or destructive behaviour against people, animals or property. Some examples include intentionally injuring others, destroying property, fire-setting, breaking some major rules of society, frequent school truancy, forced sexual activity at a young age, stealing, lying and running away from home. A child with a conduct disorder may fight a lot, bully other children or misinterpret other people's intentions as mean. They may also appear unemotional and have inadequate social skills.

Conduct disorder sets in during late childhood or early adolescence and may be mild, moderate or severe.

Behavioural/emotional disorders in children 91

The causes may be genetic or environmental. Children with ADHD are at higher risk for developing disruptive behaviour disorders and may show classroom disruption (Stormshak and Bierman, 1998). Some environmental causes are an under-controlled temperament in the family, conflict or violence in the family, poverty or parents with substance use disorder, ADHD, or mood disorder.

According to Murray and Farrington (2010), some risk factors that may predict CD and delinquency are impulsiveness, below average intelligence quotient (IQ), low scholastic achievement, inadequate parental support and improper discipline techniques, cold parental attitude, physical abuse, parents or peers displaying anti-social behaviour, low family income and a high rate of crime in the neighbourhood.

Interventions

Disruptive behaviour disorders can lead to feelings of depression, anti-social behaviour in adulthood and other mental health problems. Positive parenting and providing a safe and supportive home environment for the child can reduce the chances of children developing these disorders. Early identification and intervention are crucial in both these disorders to prevent children from displaying anti-social behaviour later in life. According to Epstein et al. (2015), interventions that are used for disruptive behaviour disorders are child-level interventions such as CBT, parent-level interventions such as the positive parenting programme (Triple P) and multi-systhemic therapy (MST).

Aggression in children

Aggressive behaviour is the observable manifestation of aggression. It is defined by Zirpoli (2008) as, "any act intended to cause harm, pain, or injury to another". It is different from violence, which is a form of physical assault. Aggressive behaviour is a broad construct that includes physical, verbal, psychological and social means of causing harm to others. It includes violent and non-violent aggressive behaviour. According to the *APA Dictionary of Psychology* (VandenBos, 2015)

aggression is behaviour aimed at harming others physically or psychologically. It can be distinguished from anger in that anger is oriented at overcoming the target but not necessarily through harm or destruction. When such behaviour is purposively performed with the primary goal of intentional injury or destruction it is termed hostile aggression. According to Sigmund Freud's classical psychoanalytical theory, the aggressive impulse is innate and derived from the death instinct. But many non-Freudian

92 *Child-adolescent behaviour*

psychoanalysts and most non psychoanalytically oriented psychologists view aggression as socially learned or as a reaction to frustration.

According to Crick and Grotpeter (1995), non-physical aggression is aggression that does not include physically harming another person. It includes:

- Verbal aggression – yelling, screaming, swearing, name-calling.
- Relational or social aggression – it is defined as intentionally harming another person's social relationships. For example, gossiping, excluding others from one's friendship or not talking to others.

Coyne and Archer (2005) argue that the reason people may use non-physical aggression instead of physical aggression is that it is subtler and they can be aggressive without showing aggression openly. According to Coyne and Archer (2005), examples of non-physical aggression include gossiping, spreading rumours, criticizing people behind their back, leaving the person out of the group, turning people against each other, dismissing others' opinions and bullying.

According to Juvonen and Gross (2008), *bullying* is a type of intimidation and causing verbal or physical harm to another. Their study revealed that the most frequent forms of online and in-school bullying involved name-calling and insults.

According to Aalsma and Brown (2008), bullying is most common in childhood and adolescence.

A child who has been bullied can experience feelings of anxiety and depression even in later life (Stapinski et al., 2014).

Craig (1998) found that children who had experienced bullying showed more depression, loneliness, peer rejection and anxiety in comparison with other children.

Sharp (1995) found that 20 per cent of adolescents in Great Britain reported being bullied by someone spreading hurtful rumours about them.

A new form of bullying in the era of technology is *"cyberbullying"*. According to Hinduja and Patchin (2015),

cyberbullying means wilful and repeated harm inflicted through the use of computers, cell phones and other electronic devices. The important elements of cyberbullying are:

- Wilful: The behaviour has to be deliberate not accidental.
- Repeated: Bullying reflects a pattern of behaviour, not just one isolated incident.
- Harm: The target must perceive that harm was inflicted.
- Computers, cell phones and other electronic devices are used. This is what differentiates cyberbullying from traditional bullying.

Ryan and Curwen's (2013) results showed that victims of cyberbullying had emotional, social and academic problems, absenteeism and school violence; emotional reactions like depression, anxiety, aggression, low self-esteem, self-harm and even suicide and poor physical health and eating disorders.

Hinduja and Patchin (2022) studied the relationship between six dimensions of parenting, i.e., warmth, structure, autonomy support, rejection, chaos and coercion in regards to school and online bullying in 12- to 17-year-old youths. Their results showed that students whose parents exhibit warmth, structure and autonomy support were less likely to have engaged in bullying and cyberbullying. Youths who had experienced rejection, chaos and coercion from parents were more likely to have engaged in bullying and cyberbullying. Hinduja and Patchin suggest that strong parent–child relationships can be used to prevent bullying.

Some possible characteristics and risk factors of aggressive behaviour of children and adolescents of different age groups are as follows (Liu et al., 2013).

Characteristics of aggressive behaviour

- Zero to two years: screaming, biting others, kicking, crying, throwing things, breaking objects.
- Two to twelve years: irritability, teasing, bullying others, cruelty to animals, fire-setting, fighting, non-verbal aggression.
- Twelve to eighteen years: gang activities, truancy, intentional destruction of property, using weapons to hurt others, stealing, dating violence, sexual assault. Defiance is another form of aggression that children exhibit such as staring at elders, making faces and doing the opposite of what they have been told to do. They express aggression verbally by shouting, yelling or threatening others and by ridiculing others.

Risk factors

- Zero to twelve years:
  - Some genetic or biological factors that may increase aggressive behaviour in children are birth complications, nutrition problems or the child's biological needs of hunger, sleep, rest or physical comfort are not satisfied. Moore et al. (2002) found that low levels of the neurotransmitter serotonin contributes to aggressive behaviours.
  - According to social learning theory (Bandura, 1977), children may imitate aggressive or violent behaviour that they see in their daily life. Aggression is a learned behaviour and the models of behaviour to which the developing child is exposed are very important (Eron et al., 1974).

94 *Child-adolescent behaviour*

- Children may show aggressive behaviour after they receive attention for it from family members, teachers or peers. Here, attention is the reward that the child gets for their behaviour. According to Skinner's theory of operant conditioning, if an action is followed by a reward, the person repeats the action (Morgan and King, 1975).
- Walters and Brown (1964) found that aggressive behaviour in children that is learned in one situation will generalize or spread to other situations if it is rewarded.
- Socio-emotional causes: Some examples are a lack of love and warmth from parents and family members, rejection by parents causing insecurity in the child, very strict or very lenient parents and parental favouritism. Blanz et al. (1991) found that poor parenting increases aggressive behaviour.
- Environmental causes: Some examples are economic problems at home, a parent with an alcohol problem or quarrelling between family members. Some other environmental causes are exposure to violence in media, that is, films, television and the internet or reading crime story books, partiality by teachers, too much pressure on the child for high marks by parents or teachers, exposure to peer group violence and experiencing physical abuse, sexual abuse or bullying.
- Twelve to eighteen years:
  - Learned aggressive behaviour from childhood carried over to adolescence. Tremblay et al. (2004) found that humans learned to regulate their use of physical aggression during preschool years. Those who did not learn this showed more chances of aggressive behaviour during adolescence and adulthood.
  - Peer pressure or competition.
  - Socio-emotional or environmental causes.
  - Adolescence-limited anti-social behaviour, which means aggressive behaviour appears only in adolescence and disappears later.
  - Emotional immaturity: Children might act aggressively when they do not know how to control/express feelings of sorrow, jealousy or anger when they cannot reach their goals.
  - Children with mental health conditions like depression, bipolar disorder or ADHD may act aggressively.

Interventions

Aggressive behaviour can be *decreased* or even *prevented* if some of the above risk factors are eliminated. Some methods that parents can use to deal with aggressive behaviour in their children are as follows:

Behavioural/emotional disorders in children 95

- If the child is very angry, parents should focus on helping them to manage anger by providing support, validating their feelings and teaching them healthy coping mechanisms.
- Children may throw temper tantrums when their demands are not fulfilled or when they have sensory meltdowns. Sensory meltdowns involve emotional outbursts like crying, refusing to cooperate etc. Some causes for sensory meltdowns are sensory overload or the child does not get what they want. Parents must divert the child's attention by engaging them in some other activities. If children are old enough to understand, parents must give clear verbal explanations.
- Children can sometimes behave in an aggressive manner to get parental attention. If parents ignore their behaviour, the behaviour may gradually reduce as the child realizes that they will not get attention. Here "attention" is positive reinforcement/reward. According to Skinner's theory of operant/instrumental conditioning, if a person's action/response does not get positive reinforcement, the likelihood of its occurrence decreases (Morgan and King, 1975).
- They should not provide a model of aggressive behaviour to their child but deal with stressful situations calmly and rationally (Bandura, 1977).
- Parents should not allow the child to read books or see films and television programmes that have a lot of violence.
- If the child is hitting and pinching others while playing, parents should give them a chance to express their grievance. They must teach the child to express their anger in a socially appropriate manner, that is, by being assertive, not aggressive.

Aggression is an act against others and causes harm to the child and to others. Aggression can involve threatening, insulting or attacking another person. Assertive behaviour involves expressing genuine feelings and standing up for one's rights (Rathus and Nevid, 2002). Assertiveness also means being competitive, confident or expressing disapproval of another's behaviour without insulting the person. This is necessary for balanced personality development.

Stuttering

According to the APA DSM-5 (2013) 'stuttering is identified as childhood-onset fluency disorder. It is also called "stammering"'. It is a speech disorder that involves a blocking, repetition or struggling with speech sounds. The speaking behaviour of the child who stutters may vary from mild difficulty with initial syllables of certain words to momentary inability to utter any sound at all. According to the *APA Dictionary of Psychology* (VandenBos, 2015)

96   *Child-adolescent behaviour*

stuttering is a disturbance in the normal fluency and time sequencing of speech. It is characterized by frequent repetition or prolongation of sounds, syllables or words, with hesitations and pauses that disrupt speech. The disorder interferes with one's ability to communicate with others, especially during stressful situations (example is public speaking), and it can be exacerbated by one's awareness of and anxiety over the dysfluency. The struggle to speak may also be accompanied by behaviours such as rapid eye blinking, trembling lips or fist clenching. By contrast, speaking in unison with another person, reading orally or singing may temporarily reduce stuttering. Its onset is between two to seven years of age. Mild cases usually recover spontaneously by the age of sixteen, but severe cases may persist into adulthood.

Craig and Tran (2006) found that children show increased stuttering when exposed to demanding stimuli or situations like speaking to a critical person such as someone in authority or a large audience. The same children may show little or no stuttering while talking to a familiar person or one who is not in authority as their anxiety is reduced.

Craig and Tran (2006) also state that most children who stutter begin to do so between two and five years of age, with the highest peak at around four years. This is called developmental stuttering. Cases of acquired stuttering occur when a person has a stroke or a trauma that causes brain injury. Some negative consequences of not speaking fluently are difficulty in establishing friendships, being bullied by classmates in school, limited vocational prospects, and in effective communication.

Symptoms

Some symptoms of stuttering according to Craig and Tran (2006) are:

- Difficulty starting a word/phrase/sentence.
- Prolonging a word/sound within a word.
- Repeating a sound/syllable/word.
- Pauses within a word (broken word), incomplete phrases.
- Addition of extra words such as "um", if difficulty moving to the next word is anticipated.
- Not being able to utter a sound for a brief time.
- Anxiety about talking especially in front of a group.
- Shyness and social avoidance behaviour.
- Physical gestures such as grimaces of the face, blinking one's eyes or jerking the head while talking.

According to Craig et al. (2009), stuttering is an involuntary fluency disorder. Their study investigated the impact of stuttering on the quality of life (QOL)

Behavioural/emotional disorders in children 97

in adults. QOL assesses the well-being of a person from a multi-dimensional perspective. Their findings indicated that stuttering has a negative impact on the person in vitality, social functioning, emotional functioning and mental health status. According to Coleman (1981), "stuttering can be stressful and self-devaluating for the stutterer". On the basis of his early experiences as a stutterer and his research in this field, Sheehan (1970) states that, "For a child or adult who has developed the problem of stuttering, the production of the spoken word can be fraught with dread and difficulty".

Causes

- If the child has a brain injury/stroke.
- Emotional stress when the child feels nervous or pressured.
- Having relatives who stutter.
- Stress in the family or high expectation from parents/teachers.

Interventions

Different coping strategies are taught to the child depending on the type and severity of the disorder. It involves the services of speech and language therapists and sometimes includes intensive teaching methods by educators trained in special education.

Craig and Tran (2006) state that to manage stuttering in adolescents and adults, firstly assessment is done of three factors: the severity of stuttering, the psychological effects and the degree of anxiety the person exhibits and assessment of social skills. To reduce stuttering, the methods used are specialized behavioural treatment to alter speech patterns and improve fluency. Dysfluency is reduced by teaching self-control techniques, giving rewards for fluency, etc. Relaxation techniques are taught to reduce anxiety and improve social skills.

Parents can help the child overcome the problem of stuttering and speak fluently in the following ways:

- They should listen to what children have to say rather than the way they say it.
- They should not interrupt them even if they have a speech block nor complete their sentence.
- Parents must make their child feel that they have all the time they need to speak out what they want to say.
- They should not tell the child to talk slowly and correctly as soon as they experience speech blocks because this increases the child's anxiety and consequently they stammer more. Stress, anxiety and fear increase stuttering.

98   *Child-adolescent behaviour*

- Methods like scolding should not be used by parents as it may worsen the problem.
- The child should not be forced to give public performances until they gain control over their speech fluency.
- Parents must speak to each other clearly and not interrupt each other. The child will then imitate that manner of speaking.
- Parents must take the child to a doctor or speech therapist:
  - If stuttering lasts for more than six months.
  - If the child shows muscle tightening or is visibly struggling to speak.
  - If it affects their ability to communicate effectively at school/work/ social interactions.
  - If it begins in adulthood.

With timely diagnosis, interventions from therapists and educators and support from parents and teachers, children with speech problems can do well in school and at work.

9 Adolescence – a crucial period

Chapter outline

- Definition
- Personality development
  - Erikson's psychosocial theory of personality development
  - Identity crisis in adolescents
- Changes during adolescence
  - Physical changes
  - Sexual adjustment
  - Social changes
  - Emotional changes
  - Mental and intellectual changes
- Role of parents
- Role of school and teachers

Definition

The word "adolescence" comes from the Latin word *"adolescere"* that means to grow to maturity. According to the *APA Dictionary of Psychology* (VandenBos, 2015),

> Adolescence is the period of human development that starts with puberty (10–12 years of age) and ends with physiological maturity (approximately 19 years of age), although the exact age span varies across individuals. During this period, major changes occur at varying rates in physical characteristics, sexual characteristics and sexual interest, resulting in significant effects on body image, self-concept and self-esteem.

It is a time of transition from childhood to adulthood. It is not only a period of rapid physical changes but also marked by changes in the individual's personality, in the social, emotional, cognitive (mental) and educational spheres. Its cultural purpose is the preparation of the adolescent for adult roles.

DOI: 10.4324/9781003373070-9

100   *Child-adolescent behaviour*

Personality development

Erikson's psychosocial theory of personality development

Erikson (1980) held that a person's social environment plays a very important role in their psychological development. According to his theory, every person goes through eight stages of development and in each stage they confront new challenges in adjustment. If the challenges are faced successfully it will lead to a good outcome. The first four stages occur in childhood and are as follows:

1. Infancy (birth to eighteen months) Challenge: Trust versus mistrust. A favourable ratio of trust and mistrust leads to hope. If the child's physical needs are met and they get love and care from their parents, they feel secure and develop an attitude of trust. If their needs are not adequately met, they develop an attitude of mistrust.
2. Babyhood (eighteen months to three years). Challenge: Autonomy versus shame and doubt. A favourable ratio of autonomy and shame and doubt leads to self-direction. The child learns new behaviours and wants to explore their surroundings. If the child is successful in directing their behaviour and encouraged by their parents, they learn to be independent. If the child's parents restrict them too much they develop a sense of doubt.
3. Early childhood (three to six years). Challenge: Initiative versus guilt. A favourable ratio of initiative and guilt leads to a sense of purpose. The child wants to take the initiative and do things. If their actions do not produce the desired results they feel guilty. If the child cannot reach their goal, they get angry. Aggressive behaviours like shouting, throwing objects when angry, can be common at this stage.
4. Middle and late childhood (six to twelve years). Challenge: Industry versus inferiority. A favourable ratio of industry and inferiority leads to competence and pleasure in work. The child acquires knowledge, learns skills and spends more time in formal education. If they master the task set by parents and teachers they feel competent, if they do not meet their expectations they feel inferior.
5. Adolescence (twelve to nineteen years). Challenge: Identity versus role confusion. A favourable ratio of identity and role confusion leads to fidelity or consistency. Identity refers to the "who am I" and "what am I going to do with my life" questions of adolescence. According to Erikson, the adolescent must establish a sense of ego identity, that is. an accrued confidence that the way one views oneself has a continuity with one's past and is matched by the perception of others. They have to decide what they want to be in terms of career, occupation, beliefs, values, attitudes and behaviour patterns. If the adolescent does not develop

Adolescence – a crucial period   101

ego identity, it leads to role confusion, that is, not knowing who they are and where they are heading in the future. This can cause anxiety.

A favourable ratio of identity to role confusion leads to the ego strength "fidelity". In Erikson's theory, "ego strengths are basic virtues that correspond with the successful resolution of each developmental stage". Fidelity is defined as "the ability to sustain loyalties freely pledged in spite of the inevitable contradictions of value systems". It emerges as a virtue at the end of the identity crisis in adolescence and indicates that a stable identity has been achieved.

Identity crisis in adolescents

This age is a very important one because it is the time when personalities and identities begin to crystallize. According to Erikson (1980), an "identity crisis" is a time of intensive analysis and exploration of different ways of looking at oneself. He held that developing a sense of identity is important during teenage years, though the formation and growth of identity is not confined to adolescence.

Identity is a trait of personality that remains consistent over time, maintains continuity and distinguishes an individual as unique. Adolescents may feel that they have to re-establish their personality to re-establish their identity. Experimentation and re-examination of identity start in two ways in the adolescent, namely, identification with a hero or hero worship and playing roles in the world of fantasy. Hero worship means they identify with a person whom they admire, maybe a teacher, friend, parent, sibling, relative, actor or athlete and start dressing, behaving or talking like them. *Egocentric tendencies* of early childhood are revived at this stage. According to the *APA Dictionary of Psychology* (VandenBos, 2015), "adolescent egocentrism is the feeling of personal uniqueness often experienced in adolescence; that is the conviction that one is special and is or should be the constant focus of others' attention". A child's thought is egocentric, which means they cannot understand another person's viewpoint. According to Elkind (1967), there is a difference between a child's and an adolescent's egocentric thoughts. An adolescent's thought is marked by egocentrism in which the adolescent can understand the thoughts of others but still has trouble separating things that are of concern to others and those that are of concern only to themselves. He holds that adolescent egocentrism is a temporary phase.

Two mental constructions that are the result of adolescent egocentrism are, "personal fables and imaginary audience". These concepts were introduced by Elkind (1967). According to the *APA Dictionary of Psychology* (VandenBos, 2015)

imaginary audience is the belief of an adolescent that others are constantly focusing attention on him or her, scrutinizing behaviours, appearance and

102 Child-adolescent behaviour

the like. The adolescent feels as though he or she is continually the central topic of interest to a group of spectators (i.e an audience) when in fact this is not the case (i.e. an imaginary audience). It is an early adolescent construct, reflective of acute self-consciousness and is considered an explanation of adolescent egocentrism.

Adolescents may see themselves as the centre of attention and assume that other people are about as preoccupied with their appearance and behaviour as they are (Milstead, 1993). The concept of imaginary audience helps to explain why adolescents are so self-conscious about their appearance and may spend long hours grooming (Elkind and Bowen, 1979).

Personal fables: According to Elkind (1967),

an adolescent's intense focus on oneself as the centre of attention is what ultimately gives rise to the belief that one is unique, and in turn, this may give rise to feelings of invulnerability. The two marked characteristics of personal fable are feelings of uniqueness and invulnerability. This complex of beliefs in the uniqueness of the adolescent's feelings and of his/ her immortality might be called a "personal fable", a story which he or she tells himself and which is not true.

This belief contributes to their illusion that they are above the rules and it may contribute to behaviour patterns such as showing off and taking risks (Cohn et al., 1995).

According to Sebastian et al. (2008), the sense of *self* changes tremendously in adolescence. This leads to some phenomena in adolescence like heightened self-consciousness and susceptibility to peer influence. Activity in the brain region associated with self-processing include the medial frontal cortex and this changes between early adolescence and adulthood. An important aspect of the self is the adolescent's self-esteem. According to Rosenberg (1965), "Self-esteem is a stable sense of personal worth or worthiness measureable by self-report. High self-esteem expresses the feeling that one is good enough. Low self-esteem implies self-dissatisfaction and lack of respect for oneself".

Body image: Having a healthy body image is an important part of a growing adolescent's self-esteem. Body image of the adolescent means how the adolescent feels or thinks about their body, physical appearance, skin, height, weight and body shape. According to the *APA Dictionary of Psychology* (VandenBos, 2015) "*Body image* means the mental picture one forms of one's body as a whole, including the physical characteristics (body percept) and one's attitudes towards these characteristics (body concept)". Adolescents can be interested in good grooming, body care, physical appearance, physical attractiveness, dresses and jewels. Some adolescents try to control their weight by dieting, others might take nutritional supplements to increase

Adolescence – a crucial period 103

their weight. They may become self-conscious and shy on account of bodily changes. Those who have negative thoughts about their bodies may show emotional reactions like low self-esteem, depression and eating disorders. This might harm their concentration in both academic and extracurricular activities. Paria et al. (2023) found that body image dissatisfaction significantly affected both rural and urban adolescent girls. There was a significant association between low self-esteem and dissatisfaction with body image. They concluded that having a negative body image lowers the person's self-esteem and this impacts the overall well-being of the person. Research by Boden et al. (2008) found that lower levels of self-esteem in adolescence were associated with a greater risk of mental health problems, substance dependence and lower levels of life and relationship satisfaction in adulthood. Sowislo and Orth (2013) found that low self-esteem contributes to depression in adolescence. Interventions should be aimed at increasing adolescents' self-esteem to reduce the risk of depression.

Changes during adolescence

There are some characteristic changes in the behaviour, attitudes and interests of adolescent children that are normal and natural at this stage and part of growing up. The changes are discussed as follows.

Physical changes

The most noticeable physical development of adolescence is a growth spurt. There is notable increase in height and weight, development of acne and pimples, increase in appetite and sleeping hours in adolescents. Puberty heralds the onset of adolescence; it is the period when the body becomes sexually mature. Puberty begins with the appearance of secondary sex characteristics such as deepening of voice; growth of body hair, moustache and beard in boys; rounding of hips and breasts and menarche in girls. There is an increase in the secretion of the hormone oestrogen in girls and testosterone in boys (Rathus and Nevid, 2002).

Sexual adjustment

According to Havighurst (1966), one developmental task of adolescence is to achieve mature relations with friends of similar age of both genders. Sexual thoughts are common in adolescence. According to Kar et al. (2015), major biological and psychological developments take place during adolescence and development of sexuality is an important bio-psycho-social development during this period. They state that the adolescent's sexual behaviour is influenced by many factors namely sex hormones, peer relations, the adolescent's nature/ temperament, the attitude of parents towards sexuality, the adolescent's

104 *Child-adolescent behaviour*

values and culture and the media that the adolescent is exposed to, attitudes of the society and cultural perception. Adolescents try to understand sexuality.

Social changes

Adolescence is an important period in social development and adolescents compare themselves with peers while developing their identity and self-concept. According to the *APA Dictionary of Psychology* (VandenBos, 2015) "major social developments take place in this period as adolescents increase their peer focus and involvement in peer related activities, place greater emphasis on social acceptance, and seek more independence and autonomy from parents".

Cohn et al. (1995) found that parents perceived drinking alcohol, smoking, failure to use seat belts and a number of other activities to be riskier than their teenagers perceived. These teenagers may not perceive these activities as risky because of their belief in the personal fable.

According to Arnett (1999), adolescence is the period in life when people are most likely to engage in risky behaviours such as risky driving, substance abuse and risky sexual behaviour. Adolescents sometimes prefer to follow the rules and values of their peer group and not those laid down by their parents as they want to become independent from their parents.

According to Galambos and Turner (1999), this striving for independence from parents sometimes leads to bickering about issues such as homework, chores, money, appearance, dating, etc. They also hold that some distancing from parents is beneficial for adolescents.

Adolescents who have close relationships with their parents and whose parents showed involvement in their schooling fare better in school, have fewer adjustment problems and are more self-reliant than those who are distant from their parents (Steinberg et al.,1992).

O'Brien and Bierman (1988) found differences between pre-adolescents and adolescents in their perception of peer groups and group influence. Pre-adolescents defined groups on the basis of common activities and social behaviour and they felt that the influence of groups was very high in these domains. Older adolescents described peer group influence as global and far-reaching and it affected their attitudes, values, appearance and illicit acts. Peer group acceptance or rejection influences self-evaluation in adolescents.

Nelson and DeBacker (2008) found that adolescents who perceived that they were respected by their classmates were more likely to report adaptive achievement motivation. Those adolescents who had a best friend who values academics showed adaptive achievement motivation.

According to Johnson et al. (2001), feelings of loneliness in adolescents were linked to problems in social interaction like social anxiety and social avoidance. Conflict between parents cause problems in adolescents like loneliness and difficulty engaging in social interaction outside the family.

Adolescence – a crucial period 105

According to *the self-determination theory by Ryan and Deci (2000)*, the satisfaction of the three *psychological needs* of competence, autonomy and relatedness is important in promoting the psychological well-being, self-motivation and social development of adolescents. These needs play an important role in various domains of the adolescent's life such as education, work, sports, maintaining friendship and teamwork. Parents and teachers play an important role in the satisfaction of these needs so that they become self-directed and self-motivated. The need for *competence* means the adolescent is able to utilize their capacities by completing challenging tasks and making use of opportunities. This gives them intrinsic satisfaction. The need for *autonomy* means the adolescent does activities that are self-chosen and makes their own decisions and takes initiative. *Relatedness* signifies how well the adolescent feels cared for, connected to and understood by significant others in their lives (family, friends, peers).

Emotional changes

Between the ages of 10 and 25, the person's brain undergoes changes that have important implications for their behaviour. Neurobiological changes that underlie social and emotional behaviour and higher cognitive functions mature in adolescence (Yurgelun-Todd, 2007). These changes in the frontal cortex are partly responsible for cognitive improvements like improvement in abstract reasoning, processing speed, affective modulation, distinguishing emotional cues and goal-directed behaviour.

According to McLaughlin et al. (2015), adolescents experience frequent and intense emotions in both positive and negative domains. Hall (1904) described adolescence as a time of "storm and stress". It refers to the decreased levels of self-control and increased levels of sensitivity that are seen in adolescents and these are due to biological changes. They experience *storm and stress in three areas*:

1. Mood disruption. Adolescents can have mood swings, that is, their emotions can change rapidly. These are the result of cognitive, environmental and hormonal changes.
2. Risky behaviour. They are more reckless and display higher rates of antisocial behaviour than other age groups. Some causes for this are emotional immaturity and peer pressure.
3. Conflict with parents. According to Hall, adolescence is a time when conflict with parents and authority figures increases.

Arnett (1999) holds that evidence supports a modified storm and stress view that gives importance to individual differences and cultural variations. Storm and stress are more likely during adolescence than at other ages but

106 *Child-adolescent behaviour*

not all adolescents experience it. It is lower in adolescents with strong traditional roots than in adolescents who are influenced by media and risk-taking peers.

Buchanan et al. (1992) suggest that hormonal changes affect activity levels, mood swings and aggressive tendencies of many adolescents, but sociocultural influences may have a greater impact.

Spencer et al. (2018) found that some causes of stress in affluent adolescent girls were experiencing pressure to perform, peer competition, differences in expectations between them and their parents and narrow constructions of success

Conte et al. (2023) studied daydreaming frequency and association with psychopathological symptoms in adolescents. Almost 13 per cent of participants showed excessive daydreaming, increased depressive and obsessive-compulsive symptoms and post-traumatic stress symptoms. They also showed conduct problems and emotional symptoms.

Uusitalo-Malmivaara (2014) measured global- and school-related happiness in young adolescents of both genders. They participated in the study at ages 12 and 15. There was a decrease in happiness in both boys and girls but more in girls. This was attributed to peer problems and, to a lesser extent, stress in school. The most important factor in increasing happiness was success in school.

Mental and intellectual changes

Adolescence is a period of rapid cognitive development. According to the *APA Dictionary of Psychology* (VandenBos, 2015), major cognitive developments that take place in adolescence are acquiring enhanced abilities to think abstractly, evaluating reality hypothetically, reconsidering prior experiences from alternate points of view, assessing data from multiple dimensions, reflecting inwardly, creating complex models of understanding and projecting complicated future scenarios.

Research by Moradi et al. (1999) showed that cognitive problems, especially memory problems, were more common in adolescents with "post-traumatic stress disorder" (PTSD). A study by Darharaj et al. (2016) found that there was significant improvement in the memory of adolescents with PTSD when they used cognitive behaviour therapy.

Piaget's theory of cognitive development

According to Piaget (1971), a child's mental development and knowledge acquisition are a result of the interaction of their maturing abilities with the external world. According to Piaget's theory, every child goes through four stages of cognitive development. A child who is in a particular stage can think about the world only in the ways possible at that stage. The stages are:

Adolescence – a crucial period 107

1. The sensory-motor stage. The first two years of life. In this stage, intelligence is manifested in action or motor responses. The child explores the environment and learns to search for missing objects. Rudimentary memory appears. By the end of this period the child manipulates the world in terms of sensory-motor schemes/solutions.

2. The pre-operational stage. Two to seven years. The child's thinking is dominated by the appearance of things, not by logic. Their language and thinking are ego-centric, that is, they cannot understand another person's viewpoint. They do not understand conservation. "Conservation" means understanding that the amount of the substance remains the same, even if its shape is changed, so long as nothing is added to it or subtracted from it.

3. The concrete operational stage. Seven to eleven years. The child's thinking is logical, bound to concrete situations; they can understand conservation. Ego-centric thought gradually disappears. The child can understand relational terms and class inclusion.

4. The formal operations stage. Eleven years to nineteen years. This stage is in adolescence and represents cognitive maturity. The adolescent is capable of using rules of logical thought, deriving rules for behaviour from general principles, testing hypotheses, focusing, understanding abstract concepts like justice, judging and deductive reasoning. Adolescents can deal with hypothetical situations, they experiment with different possibilities to determine whether their hypotheses are correct. They like to question and argue with friends' or parents' assumptions. They are capable of mental operations that transcend concrete realities.

Role of parents

To help their adolescent child to deal effectively with this transitional period, parents can bear in mind the following points:

- They must help the child to have *self-awareness* and a positive self-concept. Self-awareness means knowing one's strengths and weaknesses. Having a positive self-concept means knowing one's worth and respecting oneself. It is the driving force as to how one thinks and behaves. If adolescents have a positive self-concept they will be confident and will show good social adjustment. Gniewosz et al. (2023) found that parental warmth fosters resilience in handling social and emotional problems. This contributes to children's improved mental health.

- They should observe whether their adolescent child has negative *thoughts* about their *body* due to weight, skin colour or body shape or whether they are overusing social media. This may cause mental health conditions like depression, low self-esteem or they may have eating disorders. Parents should avoid pointing out negative physical attributes in

108 *Child-adolescent behaviour*

their child or in other people. Orth et al. (2008) found that low self-esteem contributes to depression in adolescence and young adulthood. They suggest that depression can be prevented or reduced by interventions that improve self-esteem.

- Parents must develop *healthy interests and values* in children. Value development takes place after children confirm their beliefs and truths regarding ethical/moral matters, which they have learned primarily from their parents. According to Laursen and Collins (2009), the content and quality of parent–child relationships have a significant influence on adolescents' development during and after adolescence. It affects adolescents' future relationships with their friends, spouse, teachers and other adults, their psychosocial adjustment, mental health, school performance and choice of occupation.
- Parents must help the adolescent to develop *critical thinking* skills and decision-making skills so that they can analyze information, situations and experiences in an objective manner and set realistic goals. As a result, they may be able to prevent and even handle problems better. Konowitz et al. (2023) found that mothers play an important role in helping their adolescent child to develop a sense of "purpose". Mothers served as a source of inspiration, motivating their children and providing them with support.
- They must invite the teenager's *opinion* on household matters.
- They should monitor the adolescent child's *friends* so that they can judge if the adolescent is associating with bad company.
- They must help the adolescent to decide on a course for higher studies that is in consonance with their capabilities and interests. Parents should not force the adolescent to take up a course that they like.

Role of school and teachers

High schools can prevent psychosocial problems in adolescents in the following ways:

- A programme on *vocational guidance* and *career planning* should be conducted for them in schools. They should be informed about the importance of aptitudes, potential and interest and the choice of right subjects for a particular vocation.
- Curriculum and *school programmes* should be challenging and interesting. Proper provisions for curricular, co-curricular and extra-curricular activities should be made.
- Programmes should be conducted by teachers/schools to cultivate a sense of *purpose* in adolescents. Findings by Sepulveda et al. (2021) were that adolescents had higher levels of self-efficacy and grade point average after teachers conducted a programme to develop a "sense of

Adolescence – a crucial period 109

purpose" in high school adolescents. "Purpose" is defined as a stable and generalized intention to accomplish something that is at once meaningful to the self and of consequence to the world beyond the self. A strong sense of self-efficacy regarding academic capabilities is necessary to motivate students to engage in behaviours that lead to academic achievement. Adolescents who are more purposeful are more resilient to stress, have high self-esteem, show pro-social behaviour and goal orientation and are more committed to academics.

- Adolescents must be given *assertiveness* training so that they will learn how to reduce aggressive behaviour and improve their assertiveness and social involvement. According to Hersen et al. (1984), non-assertive behaviour patterns are linked to feelings of depression. Learning to express feelings assertively has been shown to reduce depression. Simple methods to handle stressful situations must be taught to adolescents.

- Since this is a transitional phase for adolescents, they may experience mental health conditions like identity crisis, feelings of depression or stress due to parental expectations, problems with peers, etc. To cope with these problems, they may try drugs/alcohol/cigarettes or show delinquent behaviour. *Psychological counselling* by a trained counsellor should be made available in the school and college for adolescents.

References

Aalsma, M. C., & Brown, J. R. (2008). What is bullying? *Journal of Adolescent Health, 43*(2), 101–102. https://doi.org/10.1016/j.jadohealth.2008.06.001

Acosta-Gonzaga, E. (2023). The effects of self-esteem and academic engagement on university students' performance. *Behavioral Sciences, 13*(4), 348. https://doi.org/10.3390/bs13040348

Adler, A. (1928). Characteristics of the first, second and third child. *Children, the Magazine for Parents, 3*(5), 14–52.

Adler, A. (1964). *Problems of neurosis.* Harper Torchbooks.

Alfano, C. A., Ginsburg, G. S., & Kingery, J. N. (2007). Sleep-related problems among children and adolescents with anxiety disorders. *Journal of the American Academy of Child and Adolescent Psychiatry, 46*(2), 224–232. https://doi.org/10.1097/01.chi

Allport, G. W. (1961). *Pattern and growth in personality.* Holt, Reinhart & Winston.

Almeida, L. S., Prieto, L. P., Ferrando, M., Oliveira, E., & Ferrándiz, C. (2008). Torrance test of creative thinking: The question of its construct validity. *Thinking Skills and Creativity, 3*(1), 53–58. https://doi.org/10.1016/j.tsc.2008.03.003

American Academy of Pediatrics. (2006). Active healthy living: Prevention of childhood obesity through increased physical activity. *Pediatrics, 117*, 1834. http://dx.doi.org/10.1542/peds.2006-0472

American Psychiatric Association. (2013). *Diagnostic and statistical manual of mental disorders* (5th ed.). https://doi.org/10.1176/appi.books.9780890425596

Anderson-McNamee, J. K., & Bailey, S. J. (2010). The importance of play in early childhood development. *Montana State University Extension, 4*, 1–4.

Antrobus, J. S., Singer, J. L., & Greenberg, S. (1966). Studies in the stream of consciousness: Experimental enhancement and suppression of spontaneous cognitive processes. *Perceptual and Motor Skills, 23*(2), 399–417. https://doi.org/10.2466/pms.1966.23.2.399

Arasteh, J. D. (1968). Creativity and related processes in the young child: A review of the literature. *The Journal of Genetic Psychology: Research and Theory on Human Development, 112*(1), 77–108.

Arnett, J. J. (1999). Adolescent storm and stress, reconsidered. *American Psychologist, 54*(5), 317–326. https://doi.org/10.1037/0003-066X.54.5.317

Arsovski, D. (2023). The imperative for occupational therapy in children with learning disabilities. *Teacher, 26*, 41–45. https://doi.org/10.20544/teacher.26.06

Atkinson, J., & Feather, N. (1966). *A theory of achievement motivation.* Wiley and Sons.

112 References

Aunola, K., Stattin, H., & Nurmi, J.-E. (2000). Parenting styles and adolescents' achievement strategies. *Journal of Adolescence, 23*(2), 205–222. https://doi.org/10.1006/jado.2000.0308

Ayllon, T., & Azrin, N. H. (1965). The measurement and reinforcement of behavior of psychotics. *Journal of the Experimental Analysis of Behavior, 8*(6), 357–383.

Bagwell, C. L., & Schmidt, M. E. (2011). *Friendships in childhood and adolescence.* The Guilford Press.

Baird, B., Smallwood, J., Mrazek, M. D., Kam, J. W. Y., Franklin, M. S., & Schooler, J. W. (2012). Inspired by distraction: Mind wandering facilitates creative incubation. *Psychological Science, 23*(10), 1117–1122. https://doi.org/10.1177/0956797612446024

Baldwin, A. L. (1955). *Behavior and development in childhood.* Dryden Press.

Bandura, A. (1977). Self-efficacy: Toward a unifying theory of behavioral change. *Psychological Review, 84*(2), 191–215. https://doi.org/10.1037/0033-295X.84.2.191

Bandura, A. (1977). *Social learning theory.* Prentice Hall.

Bandura, A., Ross, D., & Ross, S. A. (1961). Transmission of aggressions through imitation of aggressive models. *Journal of Abnormal and Social Psychology, 63*(3), 575–582.

Banks, J. B., & Quillen, J. H. (2002). Childhood discipline: Challenges for clinicians and parents. *American Family Physician, 66*(8), 1447–1452.

Baumrind, D. (1966). Effects of authoritative parental control on child behavior. *Child Development, 37*(4), 887–907. https://doi.org/10.2307/1126611

Baumrind, D. (1991). The influence of parenting style on adolescent competence and substance use. *The Journal of Early Adolescence, 11*(1), 56–95. https://doi.org/10.1177/0272431691111004

Behere, A.P., Basnet, P., & Campbell, P. A. (2017). Effects of family structure on mental health of children: A preliminary study. *Indian Journal of Psychological Medicine, 39*, 457–463.

Beloyianni, V., & Zbainos, D. (2021). What hinders creativity? Investigating middle school students' perceived influence of barriers to creativity for improving school creativity friendliness. *Dossier—Creativity, Emotion and Education, 37*, Article ID: e81409. http://dx.doi.org/10.1590/0104-4060.81409

Berndt, T. J., & Perry, T. B. (1986). Children's perceptions of friendships as supportive relationships. *Developmental Psychology, 22*(5), 640–648. https://doi.org/10.1037/0012-1649.22.5.640

Bhatt, S., & Bahadur, A. (2018). Role of self-esteem & self-efficacy in achievement motivation among college students. *International Journal of Indian Psychology, 6*(2), 5–13. https://doi.org/10.25215/0602.061

Bhattacharya, P., & Biswas, M. (2013). *Siblings: A review on the dynamics of sibling relationship.* Radix International Education Consortium of Social Sciences, April.

Bigelow, B. J. (1977). Children's friendship expectations: A cognitive-developmental study. *Child Development, 48*(1), 246–253. https://doi.org/10.2307/1128905

Bigelsen, J., Lehrfeld, J. M., Jopp, D. S., & Somer, E. (2016). Maladaptive daydreaming: Evidence for an under-researched mental health disorder. *Consciousness and Cognition: An International Journal, 42*, 254–266. https://doi.org/10.1016/j.concog.2016.03.017

Bittner, A., Egger, H. L., Erkanli, A., Jane Costello, E., Foley, D. L., & Angold, A. (2007). What do childhood anxiety disorders predict? *Journal of Child Psychology*

References 113

and Psychiatry, and Allied Disciplines, 48, 1174–1183. https://doi.org/10.1111/j.1469-7610.2007.01812.x

Blanz, B., Schmidt, M. H., & Esser, G. (1991). Familial adversities and child psychiatric disorders. Child Psychology & Psychiatry & Allied Disciplines, 32(6), 939–950. https://doi.org/10.1111/j.1469-7610.1991.tb01921.x

Blum, N. J., Williams, G. E., Friman, P. C., & Christophersen, E. R. (1995). Disciplining young children: The role of verbal instructions and reasoning. Pediatrics, 96 2 Pt 1, 336–341.

Boden, J. M., Fergusson, D. M., & Horwood, L. J. (2008). Does adolescent self-esteem predict later life outcomes? A test of the causal role of self-esteem. Development and Psychopathology, 20(1), 319–339. https://doi.org/10.1017/S0954579408000151

Bodrova, E., & Leong, D. (2005). The importance of play: Why children need to play. Early Childhood Today, 20, 6–7.

Bosse, M.-L., Tainturier, M. J., & Valdois, S. (2007). Developmental dyslexia: The visual attention span deficit hypothesis. Cognition, 104(2), 198–230. https://doi.org/10.1016/j.cognition.2006.05.009

Briers, S. (2008). Superpowers for parents: The psychology of great parenting and happy children. Pearson/Prentice Hall.

Brown, C., & Putwain W. P. (2022). Socio-economic status, gender and achievement: The mediating role of expectancy and subjective task value. Educational Psychology, 42(6), 730–748. https://doi.org/10.1080/01443410.2021.1985083

Buchanan, C. M., Eccles, J. S., & Becker, J. B. (1992). Are adolescents the victims of raging hormones? Evidence for activational effects of hormones on moods and behavior at adolescence. Psychological Bulletin, 111(1), 62–107. https://doi.org/10.1037/0033-2909.111.1.62

Butterworth, B. (2005). The development of arithmetical abilities. Journal of Child Psychology and Psychiatry, and Allied Disciplines, 46(1), 3–18. https://doi.org/10.1111/j.1469-7610.2004.00374.x

Cairns, R. B., Cairns, B. D., Neckerman, H. J., Gest, S. D., & Gariépy, J.-L. (1988). Social networks and aggressive behavior: Peer support or peer rejection? Developmental Psychology, 24(6), 815–823. https://doi.org/10.1037/0012-1649.24.6.815

Casiano, H., Kinley, D. J., Katz, L. Y., Chartier, M. J., & Sareen, J. (2012). Media use and health outcomes in adolescents: Findings form a nationally representative survey. Journal of the Canadian Academy of Child and Adolescent Psychiatry / Journal de l'Académie canadienne de psychiatrie de l'enfant et de l'adolescent, 21(4), 296–301.

Castellucci, G., & Singla, R. (2024). Developmental Coordination Disorder (Dyspraxia). In StatPearls. StatPearls Publishing.

Chamorro-Premuzic, T. (2006). Creativity versus Conscientiousness: Which is a better predictor of student performance? Applied Cognitive Psychology, 20(4), 521–531. https://doi.org/10.1002/acp.1196

Cherry, J., McCormack, T., & Graham, A. J. (2022). The link between mind wandering and learning in children. Journal of Experimental Child Psychology, 217, 1–10. https://doi.org/10.1016/j.jecp.2021.105367

Chesters, J., & Daly, A. (2017). Do peer effects mediate the association between family socio-economic status and educational achievement? Australian Journal of Social Issues, 52(1), 63–77. https://doi.org/10.1002/ajs4.3

114 *References*

Chung, P. J., Patel, D. R., & Nizami, I. (2020). Disorder of written expression and dysgraphia: definition, diagnosis, and management. *Translational Pediatrics, 9*(Suppl 1), S46–S54. https://doi.org/10.21037/tp.2019.11.01

Cohn, L. D., Macfarlane, S., Yanez, C., & Imai, W. K. (1995). Risk-perception: Differences between adolescents and adults. *Health Psychology, 14*(3), 217–222. https://doi.org/10.1037/0278-6133.14.3.217

Coleman, J. C. (1981). *Abnormal psychology and modern life*. D B Taraporevala Sons & Company Pvt Limited, 816p.

Conte, G., Arigliani, E., Martinelli, M., Di Noia, S., Chiarotti, F., & Cardona, F. (2023). Daydreaming and psychopathology in adolescence: An exploratory study. *Early Intervention in Psychiatry, 17*(3), 263–271. https://doi.org/10.1111/eip.13323

Coopersmith, S. (1967). *The antecedents of self-esteem*. W. H. Freeman

Copeland, W. E., Keeler, G., Angold, A., & Costello, E. J. (2007). Traumatic events and posttraumatic stress in childhood. *Archives of General Psychiatry, 64*, 577–584. https://doi.org/10.1001/archpsyc.64.5.577

Corazza, G. E. (2016). Potential originality and effectiveness: The dynamic definition of creativity. *Creativity Research Journal, 28*(3), 258–267. https://doi.org/10.1080/10400419.2016.1195627

Cowell, R. A., Cicchetti, D., Rogosch, F. A., & Toth, S. L. (2015). Childhood maltreatment and its effect on neurocognitive functioning: Timing and chronicity matter. *Development and Psychopathology, 27*, 521–533.

Coyne, S. M., & Archer, J. (2005). The relationship between indirect and physical aggression on television and in real life. *Social Development, 14*(2), 324–338. https://doi.org/10.1111/j.1467-9507.2005.00304.x

Craig, A., & Tran, Y. (2006). Fear of speaking: Chronic anxiety and stammering. *Advances in Psychiatric Treatment, 12*(1), 63–68. https://doi.org/10.1192/apt.12.1.63

Craig, A., Blumgart, E., & Tran, Y. (2009). The impact of stuttering on the quality of life in adults who stutter. *Journal of Fluency Disorders, 34*(2), 61–71. https://doi.org/10.1016/j.jfludis.2009.05.002

Craig, W. M. (1998). The relationship among bullying, victimization, depression, anxiety, and aggression in elementary school children. *Personality and Individual Differences, 24*(1), 123–130. https://doi.org/10.1016/S0191-8869(97)00145-1

Crick, N. R., & Grotpeter, J. K. (1995). Relational aggression, gender, and social-psychological adjustment. *Child Development, 66*(3), 710–722. https://doi.org/10.2307/1131945

Crow, A., & Crow, L. D. (1983). *Educational psychology for teachers*. Macmillan. http://dx.doi.org/10.1111/j.1467-1770.1990.tb00954.x

Crow, L. D., & Crow, A. (1962). *Child development and adjustment: Study of child psychology*. MacMillan Co. https://doi.org/10.1037/14399-000

Cummings, E. M., & Davies, P. (1996). Emotional security as a regulatory process in normal development and the development of psychopathology. *Development and Psychopathology, 8*(1), 123–139. https://doi.org/10.1017/S0954579400007008

Cummings, E. M., & Kouros, C. D. (2008). Stress and coping. In *Encyclopedia of Infant and Early Childhood Development* (pp. 267–281). Academic Press. https://doi.org/10.1016/B978-012370877-9.00156-0

Cunningham, C. E., & Boyle, M. H. (2002). Preschoolers at risk for attention-deficit hyperactivity disorder and oppositional defiant disorder: Family, parenting, and

References 115

behavioral correlates. *Journal of Abnormal Child Psychology*, *30*(6), 555–569. https://doi.org/10.1023/A:1020855429085

Darharaj, M., Moradi, A., Hasani, J., & Amiri, H. (2016). Everyday memory in adolescents with posttraumatic stress disorder before and after treatment: Effectiveness of cognitive behavior therapy. *Advances in Cognitive Science* (Persian Journal), *18*, 56–67.

Devi, K. S. (2014). Parental disciplining and children behaviours: A review. *IOSR Journal of Humanities and Social Science, 19*, 20–25. https://doi.org/10.9790/0837 -19252025

Diagnostic and Statistical Manual of Mental Disorders, Fifth Edition, Text Revision (DSM-5-TR). (2022). American Psychiatric Association.

Döhla, D., Willmes, K., & Heim, S. (2018). Cognitive profiles of developmental Dysgraphia. *Frontiers in Psychology*, *9*, 2006. https://doi.org/10.3389/fpsyg.2018 .02006

Dominguez, O., & Carugno, P. Learning disability. [Updated 2023 Mar 19]. In StatPearls [Internet]. Treasure Island (FL): StatPearls Publishing; 2024 Jan. Available from: https://www.ncbi.nlm.nih.gov/books/NBK554371/

Donelson, E., & Gullahorn, J. E. (1977). *Women: A psychological perspective*. John Wiley & Sons.

Downey, D. B. (2001). Number of siblings and intellectual development: The resource dilution explanation. *American Psychologist, 56*(6–7), 497–504. https://doi.org/10 .1037/0003-066X.56.6-7.497

Downey, D. B., & Condron, D. J. (2004). Playing well with others in kindergarten: The benefit of siblings at home. *Journal of Marriage and Family, 66*(2), 333–350. https://doi.org/10.1111/j.1741-3737.2004.00024.x

Drevdahl, J. E. (1956). Factors of importance for creativity. *Journal of Clinical Psychology, 12*, 21–26. https://doi.org/10.1002/1097-4679(195601)12:1

Dweck, C. S. (2006). *Mindset: The new psychology of success*. Random House Publishing Group.

Elkind, D. (1967). Egocentrism in adolescence. *Child Development, 38*(4), 1025–1034. https://doi.org/10.2307/1127100

Elkind, D., & Bowen, R. (1979). Imaginary audience behavior in children and adolescents. *Developmental Psychology, 15*, 38–44. https://doi.org/10.1037/0012 -1649.15.1.38

Elmaghraby, R., & Garayalde, S. (2002). What is ADHD. American Psychiatric Association. https://www.psychiatry.org/patients-families/adhd/what-is-adhd

Epstein, R., Fonnesbeck, C., Williamson, E., et al. (2015). Psychosocial and Pharmacologic Interventions for Disruptive Behavior in Children and Adolescents [Internet]. Rockville (MD): Agency for Healthcare Research and Quality (US); (Comparative Effectiveness Reviews, No. 154). https://www.ncbi.nlm.nih.gov/ books/NBK327222/

Erickson, R. J. (1985). Play contributes to the full emotional development of the child. *Education, 105*(3), 261–263.

Erikson, E. H. (1980). *Identity and the life cycle*. W. W. Norton & Co.

Eron, L. D., Huesmann, L. R., Lefkowitz, M. M., & Walder, L. O. (1974). How learning conditions in early childhood—Including mass media—Relate to aggression in late adolescence. *American Journal of Orthopsychiatry, 44*(3), 412–423. https://doi.org /10.1111/j.1939-0025.1974.tb00894.x

116   References

Farmer, M., Échenne, B., Drouin, R., & Bentourkia, M. (2017). Insights in developmental coordination disorder. *Current Pediatric Reviews, 13*(2), 111–119. https://doi.org/10.2174/1573396313666170726113550

Ferrer-Chancy, M., & Fugate, A. (2002). The importance of friendship for school-age children. FCS2207, Series of the Department of Family, Youth and Community Sciences, Florida Cooperative Extension Service, University of Florida, IFAS, Gainesville FL 32611.

Festinger, L., Schachter, S., & Back, K. (1950). *Social pressures in informal groups; A study of human factors in housing.* Harper.

Flashman, J. (2012). Academic achievement and its impact on friend dynamics. *Sociology of Education, 85*(1), 61–80. https://doi.org/10.1177/0038040711417014

Frank, J. D. (1935). Individual differences in certain aspects of the level of aspiration. The American Journal of Psychology, 47, 119–128. https://doi.org/10.2307/1416711

Frank, J. D. (1941). Recent studies of the level of aspiration. *Psychological Bulletin, 38*(4), 218–226. https://doi.org/10.1037/h0059344

Furnham, A. (2008). *Personality and intelligence at work: Exploring and explaining individual differences at work.* Psychology Press/Taylor & Francis. https://doi.org/10.4324/9780203938911

Galambos, N. L., & Turner, P. K. (1999). Parent and adolescent temperaments and the quality of parent–adolescent relations. *Merrill-Palmer Quarterly, 45*(3), 493–511.

Gardner, J. W. (1940). The use of the term "level of aspiration". *Psychological Review, 47*(1), 59–68. https://doi.org/10.1037/h0059521

Giambra, L. M. (2000). Daydreaming characteristics across the life-span: Age differences and seven to twenty year longitudinal changes. In R. G. Kunzendorf & B. Wallace (Eds.), *Individual differences in conscious experience* (pp. 147–206). John Benjamins Publishing Company. https://doi.org/10.1075/aicr.20.08gia

Ginsburg, K. R. (2007). American Academy of Pediatrics Committee on Communications; American Academy of Pediatrics Committee on Psychosocial Aspects of Child and Family Health. The importance of play in promoting healthy child development and maintaining strong parent-child bonds. *Pediatrics, 119*(1), 182–191. https://doi.org/10.1542/peds.2006-2697

Gniewosz, G., Katstaller, M., & Gniewosz, B. (2023). Adolescents' psychological adjustment during challenging times: The role of mothers', fathers', and adolescents' ratings of parental warmth. *Developmental Psychology, 59*(1), 112–127. https://doi.org/10.1037/dev0001473

Göbel, S. M., & Snowling, M. J. (2010). Number-processing skills in adults with dyslexia. *Quarterly Journal of Experimental Psychology, 63*(7), 1361–1373. https://doi.org/10.1080/17470210903359206

Grusec, J. E., & Goodnow, J. J. (1994). Impact of parental discipline methods on the child's internalization of values: A reconceptualization of current points of view. *Developmental Psychology, 30*(1), 4–19. https://doi.org/10.1037/0012-1649.30.1.4

Hall, G. S. (1904). *Adolescence: Its psychology and its relations to physiology, anthropology, sociology, sex, crime, religion and education,* Vol. 1. D Appleton & Company. https://doi.org/10.1037/10616-000

Hamer, M., Stamatakis, E., & Mishra, G. (2009). Psychological distress, television viewing, and physical activity in children aged 4 to 12 years. *Pediatrics, 123*(5), 1263–1268. https://doi.org/10.1542/peds.2008-1523

References 117

Hammill, D. D., Leigh, J. E., McNutt, G., & Larsen, S. C. (1981). A new definition of learning disabilities. *Learning Disability Quarterly*, *4*(4), 336–342. https://doi.org /10.2307/1510735

Hancox, R. J., Milne, B. J., & Poulton, R. (2005). Association of television viewing during childhood with poor educational achievement. *Archives of Pediatrics & Adolescent Medicine*, *159*(7), 614–618.

Hartup, W. W., & Stevens, N. (1997). Friendships and adaptation in the life course. *Psychological Bulletin*, *121*(3), 355–370. https://doi.org/10.1037/0033-2909.121.3 .355

Havighurst, R. J. (1966). *Developmental tasks and education*. McKay.

Helper, M. M. (1958). Parental evaluations of children and children's self-evaluations. *The Journal of Abnormal and Social Psychology*, *56*(2), 190–194. https://doi.org /10.1037/h0039812

Hersen, M., Bellack, A. S., Himmelhoch, J. M., & Thase, M. E. (1984). Effects of social skill training, amitriptyline, and psychotherapy in unipolar depressed women. *Behavior Therapy*, *15*(1), 21–40. https://doi.org/10.1016/S0005-7894(84)80039-8

Hicks, C. G. (1980). The development of creative thinking and its relationship to IQ and reading achievement. *Reading World*, *20*(1), 44–52. https://doi.org/10.1080 /19388078009557569

Hinduja, S., & Patchin, J. W. (2015). *Bullying beyond the schoolyard: Preventing and responding to cyberbullying* (2nd Ed). Corwin.

Hinduja, S., & Patchin, J. W. (2022). Bullying and cyberbullying offending among us youth: The influence of six parenting dimensions. *Journal of Child and Family Studies*, *31*, 1454–1473. https://doi.org/10.1007/s10826-021-02208-7

Hoffman, M. L. (2000). *Empathy and moral development: Implications for caring and justice*. Cambridge University Press. https://doi.org/10.1017/CBO9780511805851

Holmes, S. J., & Robins, L. N. (1988). The role of parental disciplinary practices in the development of depression and alcoholism. *Psychiatry: Interpersonal and Biological Processes*, *51*(1), 24–36.

Hoppe, F. (1930). Untersuchungen zur Handlungs- und Affektpsychologie. IX.

Hornor, G., Bretl, D., Chapman, E., Chiocca, E., Donnell, C., Doughty, K., Houser, S., Marshall, B., Morris, K., & Quinones, S. G. (2015). Corporal punishment: Evaluation of an intervention by PNPs. *Journal of Pediatric Health Care*, *29*(6), 526–535. https://doi.org/10.1016/j.pedhc.2015.04.016

Houtz, J. C., Rosenfield, S., & Tetenbaum, T. J. (1978). Creative thinking in gifted elementary school children. *Gifted Child Quarterly*, *22*(4), 513–519.

Hurlock, E. B. (1976). *Personality development*. Tata McGraw Hill.

Hurwitz, S. C. (2002). To be successful—let them play! (For Parents Particularly). *Childhood Education*, *79*(2), 101–102.

International Dyslexia Association. (2002). Definition of Dyslexia. International Dyslexia Association. https://dyslexiaida.org/definition-of-dyslexia/

Izard, C. (1960). Personality similarity and friendship. *The Journal of Abnormal and Social Psychology*, *61*(1), 47–51. https://doi.org/10.1037/h0040056

Jankowska, D. M., & Gralewski, J. (2022). The familial context of children's creativity: parenting styles and the climate for creativity in parent–child relationship. *Creativity Studies*, *15*(1), 1–24. https://doi.org/10.3846/cs.2022.13449

Jersild A. T., Telford C. W., & James, Sawrey J. M. (1975). *Child psychology*. Prentice-Hall.

118 References

Johnson, H. D., LaVoie, J. C., & Mahoney, M. (2001). Interparental conflict and family cohesion: Predictors of loneliness, social anxiety, and social avoidance in late adolescence. *Journal of Adolescent Research, 16*(3), 304–318. https://doi.org/10.1177/0743558401163004

Johnson, J. G., Cohen, P., Smailes, E. M., Kasen, S., & Brook, J. S. (2002). Television viewing and aggressive behavior during adolescence and adulthood. *Science, 295*(5564), 2468–2471. https://doi.org/10.1126/science.1062929

Joshi, S., & Srivastava, R. (2009). Self-esteem and academic achievement of adolescents. *Journal of the Indian Academy of Applied Psychology, 35*, 33–39.

Juvonen, J., and Gross, E. F. (2008). Extending the school grounds? – Bullying experiences in cyberspace. *J Sch Health., 78*(9), 496–505. https://doi.org/10.1111/j.1746-1561.2008.00335.x

Kar, S. K., Choudhury, A. S., & Singh, A. P. (2015). Understanding normal development of adolescent sexuality: A bumpy ride. *Journal of Human Reproductive Sciences, 8*, 70–74.

Karwowski, M., Gralewski, J., Patston, T., Cropley, D. H., & Kaufman, J. C. (2020). The creative student in the eyes of a teacher: A cross-cultural study. *Thinking Skills and Creativity, 35*, Article 100636. https://doi.org/10.1016/j.tsc.2020.100636

Kaufman, J. C., & Beghetto, R. A. (2009). Beyond big and little: The four c model of creativity. *Review of General Psychology, 13*(1), 1–12. https://doi.org/10.1037/a0013688

Kennedy-Moore, E., & McLaughlin, C. (2017). *Growing friendships: A kids' guide to making and keeping friends.* Simon & Schuster.

Kertechian, S. K. (2018). Conscientiousness as a key to success for academic achievement among French university students enrolled in management studies. *The International Journal of Management Education, 16*(2), 154–165. https://doi.org/10.1016/j.ijme.2018.02.003

Killingsworth, M. A., & D. T. Gilbert. (2010). A wandering mind is an unhappy mind. *Science, 330*(6006), 932–932. https://doi.org/10.1126/science.1192439

Klinger, E. (1990). *Daydreaming: Using waking fantasy and imagery for self-knowledge and creativity.* J. P. Tarcher.

Konowitz, L., Lund, T., Chia, S. W. C., Reed, M., Wood, W., Liang, B., Blustein, D., & Barnett, M. (2023). The powerful role of mothers in adolescent purpose development. *Journal of Psychological Research, 5*(1). https://doi.org/10.30564/jpr.v5i1.5236

Kucian, K., Zuber, I., Kohn, J., Poltz, N., Wyschkon, A., Esser, G., & von Aster, M. (2018). Relation between mathematical performance, math anxiety, and affective priming in children with and without developmental dyscalculia. *Frontiers in Psychology, 9*. https://doi.org/10.3389/fpsyg.2018.00263

Ladd, G. W., Kochenderfer, B. J., & Coleman, C. C. (1997). Classroom peer acceptance, friendship, and victimization: Distinct relational systems that contribute uniquely to children's school adjustment? *Child Development, 68*(6), 1181–1197. https://doi.org/10.2307/1132300

Landerl, K., & Moll, K. (2010). Comorbidity of learning disorders: Prevalence and familial transmission. *Journal of Child Psychology and Psychiatry, and Allied Disciplines, 51*(3), 287–294. https://doi.org/10.1111/j.1469-7610.2009.02164.x

Laursen, B., & Collins, W. A. (2009). Parent-child relationships during adolescence. In R. M. Lerner & L. Steinberg (Eds.), *Handbook of adolescent psychology:*

References 119

Contextual influences on adolescent development (3rd ed., pp. 3–42). John Wiley & Sons, Inc. https://doi.org/10.1002/9780470479193.adlpsy002002

Leman, K. (1982). *The birth order book: Why you are the way you are*. F.H. Revell.

Lindgren, H. C. (1973). *An introduction to social psychology*. Wiley.

Liu, J., Lewis, G. D., & Evans, L. K. (2013). Understanding aggressive behaviour across the lifespan. *Journal of Psychiatric and Mental Health Nursing, 20*(2), 156–168.

Lucas, B. (2001). Creative teaching, teaching creativity and creative learning. In A. Craft, B. Jeffrey & M. Liebling (Eds.), *Creativity in Education* (pp. 35–44). Continuum.

Maccoby, E. E., & Martin, J. A. (1983). Socialization in the context of the family: Parent-child interaction. In P. H. Mussen & E. M. Hetherington (Eds.), *Handbook of child psychology: Vol. 4. Socialization, personality, and social development* (pp. 1–101). Wiley.

Margolis, H., & Mccabe, P. P. (2006). Improving self-efficacy and motivation: What to do, what to say. *Intervention in School and Clinic, 41*(4), 218–227. https://doi.org /10.1177/10534512060410040401

Maslow, A. H. (1943). A theory of human motivation. *Psychological Review, 50*(4), 370–396. https://doi.org/10.1037/h0054346

Massie, M.-H., Puozz o, I. C., & Boutet, M. (2022). Teacher creativity: When professional coherence supports beautiful risks. *Journal of Intelligence, 10*(3), 1–16. https://doi.org/10.3390/jintelligence10030062

Mathijs, L., Mouton, B., Zimmermann, G., & Van Petegem, S. (2023). Overprotective parenting and social anxiety in adolescents: The role of emotion regulation. *Journal of Social and Personal Relationships, 0*(0). https://doi.org/10.1177 /02654075231173722

McAnally, H. M., Young, T. R., & Hancox, R. J. (2019). Childhood and adolescent television viewing and internalising disorders in adulthood. *Preventive Medicine Reports, 15.*

McClelland, D. C. (1987). *Human motivation*. Cambridge University Press.

McLaughlin, K. A., Garrad, M. C., & Somerville, L. H. (2015). What develops during emotional development? A component process approach to identifying sources of psychopathology risk in adolescence. *Dialogues in Clinical Neuroscience, 17*(4), 403–410. https://doi.org/10.31887/DCNS.2015.17.4

Meachon, E. J., Zemp, M., & Alpers, G. W. (2022). Developmental Coordination Disorder (DCD): Relevance for clinical psychologists in Europe. *Clinical Psychology in Europe, 4*(2), 1–24. https://doi.org/10.32872/cpe.4165

Merry, J., Bobbitt-Zeher, D., & Downey, D. (2020). Number of siblings in childhood, social outcomes in adulthood. *Journal of Family Issues, 41*(2), 212–234. https://doi .org/10.1177/0192513x19873356

Miller, D. R. (1963). The study of social relationships: Situation, identity, and social interaction. In S. Koch (Ed.), *Psychology: A study of a science* (Vol. 5). McGraw-Hill.

Miller, T. W. (1971). Communicative dimensions of mother-child interaction as they affect the self-esteem of the child. *Proceedings of the Annual Convention of the American Psychological Association, 6*(Pt. 1), 241–242.

Milstead, M. (1993). Interpersonal understanding, separation–individuation, and imaginary audience and personal fable: A test of an integrated model for early

120 References

and middle adolescence. *Dissertation Abstracts International, 54*(03), 1695A. (University Microfilms No. DA93-20190).

Mohanty, G. (1978). Sex differences in shifts and rigidity in level of aspiration experiments. *Journal of Psychological Researches, 22*(1), 18–20.

Moore, T. M., Scarpa, A., & Raine, A. (2002). A meta-analysis of serotonin metabolite 5-HIAA and antisocial behavior. *Aggressive Behavior, 28*(4), 299–316. https://doi.org/10.1002/ab.90027

Moradi, A. R., Doost, H. T. N., Taghavi, M. R., Yule, W., & Dalgleish, T. (1999). Everyday memory deficits in children and adolescents with PTSD: Performance on the Rivermead Behavioural Memory Test. *Journal of Child Psychology and Psychiatry, 40*(3), 357–361. https://doi.org/10.1111/1469-7610.00453

Morgan Clifford Thomas and Richard Austin King. (1975). *Study guide for Morgan and King introduction to psychology: Fifth Edition.* McGraw-Hill.

Murray, J., & Farrington, D. P. (2010). Risk factors for conduct disorder and delinquency: Key findings from longitudinal studies. *The Canadian Journal of Psychiatry, 55*, 633–642.

National Institute of Mental Health. (2024). https://www.nimh.nih.gov/health/topics/anxiety-disorders

Nelson, R. M., & DeBacker, T. K. (2008). Achievement motivation in adolescents: The role of peer climate and best friends. *Journal of Experimental Education, 76*(2), 170–189. https://doi.org/10.3200/JEXE.76.2.170-190

Nieman, P., Shea, S., & Canadian Paediatric Society, Community Paediatrics Committee. (2004). Effective discipline for children. *Paediatrics & Child Health, 9*(1), 37–41. https://doi.org/10.1093/pch/9.1.37

O'Brien, S. F., & Bierman, K. L. (1988). Conceptions and perceived influence of peer groups: Interviews with preadolescents and adolescents. *Child Development, 59*(5), 1360–1365. https://doi.org/10.2307/1130498

Ogundele, M. O. (2018). Behavioural and emotional disorders in childhood: A brief overview for paediatricians. *World Journal of Clinical Pediatrics, 7*, 9–26.

Oliva, A., & Arranz, E. (2005). Sibling relationships during adolescence. *European Journal of Developmental Psychology, 2*(3), 253–270. https://doi.org/10.1080/17405620544000002

Orth, U., Robins, R. W., & Roberts, B. W. (2008). Low self-esteem prospectively predicts depression in adolescence and young adulthood. *Journal of Personality and Social Psychology, 95*(3), 695–708. https://doi.org/10.1037/0022-3514.95.3.695

Ottaviani, C., & Couyoumdjian, A. (2013). Pros and cons of a wandering mind: A prospective study. *Frontiers in Psychology, 4*, 524. https://doi.org/10.3389/fpsyg.2013.00524

Owens, J. A., Maxim, R. A., McGuinn, M., Nobile, C., Msall, M. E., & Alario, A. J. (1999). Television-viewing habits and sleep disturbance in school children. *Pediatrics, 104*, e27–e27.

Öztürk, N. (2019). Assessing the friendship quality of children between the ages of 9 and 12 based on certain variables. *International Journal of Academic Research in Education, 5*(1–2), 9–24. https://doi.org/10.17985/ijare.599837

Paria, B., Dwivedi, M., & Roy, S. K. (2023). A cross-sectional study on body image perception and self-esteem among adolescent girls in urban and rural areas of Kolkata, West Bengal, India. *Journal of Clinical and Diagnostic Research, 17*(11), LC11–LC14. https://doi.org/10.7860/JCDR/2023/62667.18697

References   121

Parker, J., & Seal, J. (1996). Forming, losing, renewing, and replacing friendships: Applying temporal parameters to the assessment of children's friendship experiences. *Child Development, 67,* 2248–2268. https://doi.org/10.1111/j.1467 -8624.1996.tb01855.x

Paul, E. L., & Brier, S. (2001). Friendsickness in the transition to college: Precollege predictors and college adjustment correlates. *Journal of Counseling & Development, 79*(1), 77–89. https://doi.org/10.1002/j.1556-6676.2001.tb01946.x

Paulhus, D. L., Trapnell, P. D., & Chen, D. (1999). Birth order effects on personality and achievement within families. *Psychological Science, 10*(6), 482–488. https://doi.org/10.1111/1467-9280.00193

Pearson, J. L., Ialongo, H. S., Hunter, A. G., & Kellum, S. G. (1994). Family structure and aggressive behavior in a population of urban elementary school children. *Journal of the American Academy of Child and Adolescent Psychiatry, 33,* 540–548.

Pellegrini, A. D., & Smith, P. K. (1998). The development of play during childhood: Forms and possible functions. *Child Psychology & Psychiatry Review, 3*(2), 51–57. https://doi.org/10.1017/S1360641798001476

Pervin, L. A. (1980). *Personality: Theory, assessment, and research.* Wiley & Sons.

Piaget, J. (1962). *Play dreams and imitation in childhood.* W. W. Norton.

Piaget, J. (1971). The theory of stages in cognitive development. In D. R. Green, M. P. Ford, & G. B. Flamer (Eds.), *Measurement and Piaget* (pp. 1–11) McGraw-Hill.

Poulin, F., & Chan, A. (2010). Friendship stability and change in childhood and adolescence. *Developmental Review, 30*(3), 257–272. https://doi.org/10.1016/j.dr .2009.01.001

Prabhakararao, S. (2016). Overuse of social media affects the mental health of adolescents and early youth. *The International Journal of Indian Psychology, 3*(2), No. 8, 14–19. https://doi.org/18.01.136/20160302

Pranjić, M., Rahman, N., Kamenetskiy, A., Mulligan, K., Pihl, S., & Arnett, A. B. (2023). A systematic review of behavioral and neurobiological profiles associated with coexisting attention-deficit/hyperactivity disorder and developmental coordination disorder. *Neuroscience and Biobehavioral Reviews, 153,* 105389. https://doi.org/10.1016/j.neubiorev.2023.105389

Pressey, S. L. (1960). Toward earlier creativity in psychology. *American Psychologist, 15*(2), 124–127. https://doi.org/10.1037/h0044900

Primack, B. A., Swanier, B., Georgiopoulos, A. M., Land, S. R., & Fine, M. J. (2009). Association between media use in adolescence and depression in young adulthood: A longitudinal study. *Archives of General Psychiatry, 66*(2), 181–188. https://doi .org/10.1001/archgenpsychiatry.2008.532

Rathus, S. A., & Nevid, J. S. (2002). *Psychology and challenges of life* (8th ed.). John Wiley & Sons.

Reid Chassiakos, Y. L., Radesky, J. S., Christakis, D. A., Moreno, M. A., & Cross, C. (2016). Children and adolescents and digital media. *Pediatrics, 138*(5), e20162593. https://doi.org/10.1542/peds.2016-2593

Repetti, R. L., Taylor, S. E., & Seeman, T. E. (2002). Risky families: Family social environments and the mental and physical health of offspring. *Psychological Bulletin, 128*(2), 330–366. https://doi.org/10.1037/0033-2909.128.2.330

Richardson, M., & Abraham, C. (2009). Conscientiousness and achievement motivation predict performance. *European Journal of Personality, 23*(7), 589–605. https://doi .org/10.1002/per.732

122 References

Rimrodt, S. L., & Lipkin, P. H. (2011). Learning disabilities and school failure. *Pediatrics in Review, 32*(8), 315–324. https://doi.org/10.1542/pir.32-8-315

Robertson, L., McAnally, H. M., & Hancox, R. J. (2013). Childhood and adolescent television viewing and antisocial behavior in early adulthood. *Pediatrics, 131*, 439–446.

Robins, R. W., Hendin, H. M., & Trzesniewski, K. H. (2001). Measuring global self-esteem: Construct validation of a single-item measure and the Rosenberg Self-Esteem Scale. *Personality and Social Psychology Bulletin, 27*(2), 151–161. https://doi.org/10.1177/0146167201272002

Rogers, C. R. (1951). *Client-centered therapy; its current practice, implications, and theory.* Houghton Mifflin.

Rogers, M. A., Theule, J., Ryan, B. A., Adams, G. R., & Keating, L. (2009). Parental involvement and children's school achievement: Evidence for mediating processes. *Canadian Journal of School Psychology, 24*(1), 34–57. https://doi.org/10.1177/0829573508328445

Romano, E., Babchishin, L., Marquis, R., & Fréchette, S. (2015). Childhood maltreatment and educational outcomes. *Trauma, Violence, & Abuse, 16*(4), 418–437. https://doi.org/10.1177/1524838014537908

Rosenberg, M. (1965). *Society and the adolescent self-image.* Princeton University Press.

Ryan, K. N., & Curwen, T. (2013). Cyber-victimized students: Incidence, impact, and intervention. *Sage Open, 3*(4). https://doi.org/10.1177/2158244013516772

Ryan, R. M., & Deci, E. L. (2000). Self-determination theory and the facilitation of intrinsic motivation, social development, and well-being. *American Psychologist, 55*(1), 68–78. https://doi.org/10.1037/0003-066X.55.1.68

Sebastian, C., Burnett, S., & Blakemore, S.-J. (2008). Development of the self-concept during adolescence. *Trends in Cognitive Sciences, 12*(11), 441–446. https://doi.org/10.1016/j.tics.2008.07.008

Sege, R. D., & Siegel, B. S. (2018). Effective discipline to raise healthy children. *Pediatrics, 142*(6), e20183112. https://doi.org/10.1542/peds.2018-3112

Selvitopu, A., & Kaya, M. (2021). A meta-analytic review of the effect of socioeconomic status on academic performance. *Journal of Education, 203*(4), 768–780. https://doi.org/10.1177/00220574211031978

Sepulveda, J. A., Lincoln, B., Liang, B., Klein, T., White, A. E., Hill, N., & Perella, J. (2021). MPOWER: The impact of a purpose program on adolescents' intrinsic and extrinsic motivations. *Frontiers in Psychology, 12.* https://doi.org/10.3389/fpsyg.2021.761580

Sharp, S. (1995). How much does bullying hurt? The effects of bullying on the personal wellbeing and educational progress of secondary aged students. *Educational and Child Psychology, 12*(2), 81–88.

Sheehan, J. G. (1970). *Stuttering: Research and therapy.* Harper & Row.

Shinohara, R., Sugisawa, Y., Tong, L., Tanaka, E., Watanabe, T., Onda, Y., Kawashima, Y., Hirano, M., Tomisaki, E., Mochizuki, Y., Morita, K., Amarsanaa, G., Yato, Y., Yamakawa, N., & Anme, T. (2012). Influence of maternal praise on developmental trajectories of early childhood social competence. *Creative Education, 3*, 533. https://dx.doi.org/10.4236/ce.2012.34081

Sing, L., Apple, C.Y. Au, Toby, M. Y. Tong, Jelena, C. Y. Poon, & Julia, W. S. Wan. (2023). parental attitudes and behaviors and children's creativity. *International Journal of Social Work, 10*(1), 102–124.

References 123

Singer, J. L. (1998). Daydreams, the stream of consciousness, and self-representations. In R. F. Bornstein & J. M. Masling (Eds.), *Empirical perspectives on the psychoanalytic unconscious* (pp. 141–186). American Psychological Association. https://doi.org/10.1037/10256-005

Singer, J. L. (1975). *Daydreaming and fantasy* (Psychology Revivals) (1st ed.). Routledge. https://doi.org/10.4324/9781315778679

Skinner, B. F. (1968). *The technology of teaching*. Appleton-Century-Crofts.

Smallwood, J., & Schooler, J. W. (2015). The science of mind wandering: Empirically navigating the stream of consciousness. *Annual Review of Psychology, 66*, 487–518.

Smith, D. S. (1995). How play influences children's development at home and school. *The Journal of Physical Education, Recreation & Dance, 66*, 19–23.

Snowling, M. J., Hayiou-Thomas, M. E., Nash, H. M., & Hulme, C. (2020a). Dyslexia and Developmental Language Disorder: Comorbid disorders with distinct effects on reading comprehension. *Journal of Child Psychology and Psychiatry, and Allied Disciplines, 61*(6), 672–680. https://doi.org/10.1111/jcpp.13140

Snowling, M. J., Hulme, C., & Nation, K. (2020b). Defining and understanding dyslexia: Past, present and future. *Oxford Review of Education, 46*(4), 501–513. https://doi.org/10.1080/03054985.2020.1765756

Soares, N., Evans, T., & Patel, D. R. (2018). Specific learning disability in mathematics: A comprehensive review. *Translational Pediatrics, 7*(1), 48–62. https://doi.org/10.21037/tp.2017.08.03

Soemer, A., Gericke, C., & Schiefele, U. (2022). Does mind wandering mediate the effects of habitual reading motivation on comprehension? *Learning and Instruction, 83*. https://doi.org/10.1016/j.learninstruc.2022.101693

Somer, E. (2002). Maladaptive daydreaming: A qualitative inquiry. *Journal of Contemporary Psychotherapy: On the Cutting Edge of Modern Developments in Psychotherapy, 32*(2–3), 197–212. https://doi.org/10.1023/A:1020597026919

Sowislo, J. F., & Orth, U. (2013). Does low self-esteem predict depression and anxiety? A meta-analysis of longitudinal studies. *Psychological Bulletin, 139*, 213–240. http://dx.doi.org/10.1037/a0028931

Spencer, R., Walsh, J., Liang, B., Mousseau, A. M. D., & Lund, T. J. (2018). Having it all? A qualitative examination of affluent adolescent girls' perceptions of stress and their quests for success. *Journal of Adolescent Research, 33*(1), 3–33. https://doi.org/10.1177/0743558416670990

Stapinski, L. A., Bowes, L., Wolke, D., Pearson, R. M., Mahedy, L., Button, K. S., Lewis, G., & Araya, R. (2014). Peer victimization during adolescence and risk for anxiety disorders in adulthood: A prospective cohort study. *Depression and Anxiety, 31*(7), 574–582. https://doi.org/10.1002/da.22270

Starovoytova, D., & Arimi, M. E. (2017). Witnessing of cheating-in-exams behavior and factors sustaining integrity. *Journal of Education and Practice, 8*, 127–141.

Stawarczyk, D., Majerus, S., Catalem C., & D'Argembeaum, A. (2014). Relationships between mind-wandering and attentional control abilities in young adults and adolescents. *Acta Psychologica* (Amst), *148,* 25–36. https://doi.org/10.1016/j.actpsy.2014.01.007

Stein, D. J., Craske, M. A., Friedman, M. J., & Phillips, K. A. (2014). Anxiety disorders, obsessive-compulsive and related disorders, trauma- and stressor-related disorders, and dissociative disorders in DSM-5. *American Journal of Psychiatry, 171*(6), 611–613. https://doi.org/10.1176/appi.ajp.2014.14010003

124 References

Steinberg, L., Lamborn, S. D., Dornbusch, S. M., & Darling, N. (1992). Impact of parenting practices on adolescent achievement: Authoritative parenting, school involvement, and encouragement to succeed. *Child Development, 63*(5), 1266–1281. https://doi.org/10.2307/1131532

Sternberg, R. J., & Lubart, T. I. (1991). An investment theory of creativity and its development. *Human Development, 34*, 1–34. https://doi.org/10.1159/000277029

Stormshak, E. A, & Bierman, K. L. (1998). The implications of different developmental patterns of disruptive behavior problems for school adjustment. Conduct Problems Prevention Research Group. *Developmental Psychopathology, 10*(3), 451–467. https://doi.org/10.1017/s0954579498001692

Straus, M. A., Sugarman, D. B., & Giles-Sims, J. (1997). Spanking by parents and subsequent antisocial behavior of children. *Archives of Pediatrics & Adolescent Medicine, 151*(8), 761–767.

Suitor, J. J., Sechrist, J., Plikuhn, M., Pardo, S. T., Gilligan, M., & Pillemer, K. (2009). The role of perceived maternal favoritism in sibling relations in midlife. *Journal of Marriage and Family, 71*(4), 1026–1038. https://doi.org/10.1111/j.1741-3737.2009 .00650.x

Sulloway, F. J. (1996). *Born to rebel: Birth order, family dynamics, and creative lives.* Pantheon Books.

Sulloway, F. J. (1998). How is personality formed? A talk with Frank J. Sulloway. https://www.edge.org/conversation/frank_j_sulloway-how-is-personality-formed (accessed on January 24, 2024).

Tamis-LeMonda, C. S., Shannon, J. D., Cabrera, N. J., & Lamb, M. E. (2004). Fathers and mothers at play with their 2- and 3-year-olds: Contributions to language and cognitive development. *Child Development, 75*(6), 1806–1820. https://doi.org/10 .1111/j.1467-8624.2004.00818.x

Taylor, C. A., Manganello, J. A., Lee, S. J., & Rice, J. C. (2010). Mothers' spanking of 3-year-old children and subsequent risk of children's aggressive behavior. *Pediatrics, 125*, e1057–e1065.

Thorndike, E. L. (1903). *Educational psychology.* Lemcke & Buechner. https://doi.org /10.1037/10528-000

Tremblay, R. E., Nagin, D. S., Séguin, J. R., Zoccolillo, M., Zelazo, P. D., Boivin, M., Pérusse, D., & Japel, C. (2004). Physical aggression during early childhood: Trajectories and predictors. *Pediatrics, 114*(1), e43–e50. https://doi.org/10.1542/ peds.114.1.e43

Trent, K., & Spitze, G. (2011). Growing up without siblings and adult sociability behaviors. *Journal of Family Issues, 32*(9), 1178–1204. https://doi.org/10.1177 /0192513X11398945

Tsao, L. (2002). How much do we know about the importance of play in child development? *Review of Research. Childhood Education, 78*(4), 230–233.

Tsitsani, P., Psyllidou, S., Batzios, S., Livas, S. S., Ouranos, M., & Cassimos, D. C. (2012). Fairy tales: A compass for children's healthy development—a qualitative study in a Greek island. *Child: Care, Health and Development, 38*(2), 266–272.

Unsworth, N., & McMillan, B. D. (2013). Mind wandering and reading comprehension: Examining the roles of working memory capacity, interest, motivation, and topic experience. *Journal of Experimental Psychology: Learning, Memory, and Cognition, 39*(3), 832–842. https://doi.org/10.1037/a0029669

References   125

Uusitalo-Malmivaara, L. (2014). Happiness decreases during early adolescence—A study on 12- and 15-year-old Finnish students. *Psychology, 5*, 541–555. https://doi.org/10.4236/psych.2014.56064

VandenBos, G. R. (Ed.). (2015). *APA dictionary of psychology* (2nd ed.). American Psychological Association. https://doi.org/10.1037/14646-000

Verbree, A. R., Hornstra, L., Maas, L., & Wijngaards-de Meij, L. (2023). Conscientiousness as a predictor of the gender gap in academic achievement. *Research in Higher Education, 64*(3), 451–472. https://doi.org/10.1007/s11162-022-09716-5

Verenikina, I., Harris, P., & Lysaght, P. (2003). Child's play: Computer games, theories of play and children's development. *CRPIT '03: Proceedings of the International Federation for Information Processing Working Group 3.5, Open Conference on Young Children and Learning Technologies, 34*, 99–106.

Vissing, Y. M., Straus, M. A., Gelles, R. J., & Harrop, J. W. (1991). Verbal aggression by parents and psychosocial problems of children. *Child Abuse & Neglect, 15*(3), 223–238. https://doi.org/10.1016/0145-2134(91)90067-N

Walters, Richard H., & Ralph Brown, M. (1964). A test of the high-magnitude theory of aggression. *Journal of Experimental Child Psychology, 1*, 376–387.

Wankat, P. C., & Oreovicz, F. S. (2015). *Teaching engineering* (2nd ed.). Purdue University Press. https://doi.org/10.2307/j.ctv15wxqn9

Wolraich, M. L., et al. (2019). Clinical practice guideline for the diagnosis, evaluation, and treatment of attention-deficit/hyperactivity disorder in children and adolescents. *Pediatrics, 144*(4), e20192528. https://doi.org/10.1542/peds.2019-2528

Xiaoxia Ai. (1999). Creativity and academic achievement: An investigation of gender differences. *Creativity Research Journal, 12*(4), 329–337. https://doi.org/10.1207/s15326934crj1204_11

Yabe, M., Oshima, S., Eifuku, S., Taira, M., Kobayashi, K., Yabe, H., & Niwa, S. (2018). Effects of storytelling on the childhood brain: Near-infrared spectroscopic comparison with the effects of picture-book reading. *Fukushima Journal of Medical Science, 64*(3), 125–132.

Yang, J., Hou, X., Wei, D., Wang, K., Li, Y., & Qiu, J. (2017). Only-child and non-only-child exhibit differences in creativity and agreeableness: Evidence from behavioral and anatomical structural studies. *Brain Imaging and Behavior, 11*(2), 493–502. https://doi.org/10.1007/s11682-016-9530-9

Yeh, Yu-chu, & Ting, Yu-Shan. (2023). Comparisons of creativity performance and learning effects through digital game-based creativity learning between elementary school children in rural and urban areas. *The British Journal of Educational Psychology, 93*(3), 790–805. https://doi.org/10.1111/bjep.12594

Yurgelun-Todd, D. (2007). Emotional and cognitive changes during adolescence. *Current Opinion in Neurobiology, 17*(2), 251–257. https://doi.org/10.1016/j.conb.2007.03.009

Zirpoli, T. J. (2008). *Behavior management: Applications for teachers*. Pearson/Merrill Prentice Hall.

Index

aggression 14, 28, 31, 38–40, 44, 78, 81, 84, 91–5
anxious 3, 38, 44, 74, 87–9
assertive 40, 54, 95, 109
autonomy 9, 44, 56, 62–3, 93, 100, 104–5

behaviour disorders 71, 80–2, 89, 91
birth order 13–14
body image 99, 102–3
brain storm 63–4
bullying 32, 78, 92–4

competence 5, 7–8, 28, 43–4, 52, 56, 100, 105
conduct disorder 81, 89–90
conquering hero 35
conscientiousness 14, 49, 51, 53–4, 65
creative thinking 34, 58–60, 64–6
cyberbullying 92–3

daydreams 20–1, 34–5
demandingness 44
developmental coordination disorder 75
dyscalculia 70–1, 73–4, 78
dysgraphia 70–2, 78
dyslexia 70–2, 74, 78

egocentrism 101–2
emotional intelligence 30, 61
emotional security 6–7, 9, 16, 27,42

favouritism 17–18, 94
fear of failure 65

flexibility 15, 49, 58–60, 62, 64
fluency 58–60, 64, 70–1, 74, 78, 86, 95–8
focussed attention 41
friendship 13, 24–8, 92, 105

heredity 2–4, 61
hyperactivity 72, 76, 81–3

identification 2, 10, 41, 53, 77–8, 82, 89, 91, 101
identity 2, 24–5, 27–8, 32, 100–1, 104, 109
imaginary audience 101–2
impulsivity 82–4
inattention 82–3
intellectual thinking 60

learning disabilities 69–70, 72, 77–9
level of aspiration 47–9, 51, 56

maladjusted 49
media: digital 32; mass 3, 5, 31, 49; print 20, 29; social 3, 20, 21, 32, 107
mind-wandering 33–4

need for: achievement 48, 50–2, 54; affiliation 50; power 50
neurodevelopmental 69, 74–5

ordinal position 11, 13, 62
originality 58–9, 64
overprotection 8–9

Index 127

parenting style: authoritarian 43;
authoritative 43–4; constructive
62; neglectful 43; permissive 43
peer: group 3, 27, 62, 94, 104;
pressure 28, 65, 94, 105
permissiveness 9
personal fable 101–2, 104
phobia 86–8
positive reinforcement 37–8, 40,
45, 95
praise 17, 37–8, 41–5, 56–7, 64,
89
propinquity 26
psychological counselling 109
psychological needs 7, 49, 105
puberty 99, 103
punishment 7, 10, 36–43, 45, 49, 52,
57, 68, 89
purpose 38, 51, 90, 99–100, 108–9

rejection 9,27,92–4, 104
relatedness 105
resilience 23, 41, 44, 64, 107
responsiveness 44
reward 36–8, 45, 66, 68, 94–5
role models 29, 41, 53

self: actualization 6, 8; awareness
107; concept 1–2, 4–5, 11, 28,
99, 104, 107; efficacy 5, 49, 51,
55–7, 65, 108–9; esteem 2, 5,
7–8, 15, 17, 22, 27, 38–9, 44,
49, 54–56, 77, 79, 93, 99,102–3,
107–9; evaluation 5, 57, 104;
ideal 5
sibling rivalry 12, 14, 17–19

similarity 25–7
social: anxiety 9, 35, 86, 88, 104;
networking sites (SNS) 32; skills
7, 10, 15–16, 21–2, 28–9, 31–2,
90, 97
socio-emotional 7, 27, 71, 94
stuttering 95–8
suffering martyr 35
supportive climate 61, 65–6

techniques: motivational 56; power-
oriented 40,45
theory of: achievement motivation
50; cognitive development 106;
creativity and its development
61; emotional security 9;
friendship 26; human motivation
7; learning 68; needs 50; operant/
instrumental conditioning 37, 68,
94–5; psychosocial development
100; self-determination 105;
social learning 10, 93
time-out 37, 41, 94
traits 1–3, 5, 14, 17, 26, 28, 31, 51,
53, 64
transition 5, 99
types of play: constructive 22,
expressive 22, motor 22, pretend
23, 63

verbal: aggression 38, 92;
explanation 37–8; punishment
38–9, 40–1, 45
vocational guidance 108

well-adjusted 49